This Man and Music

ALSO BY ANTHONY BURGESS

novels

The Long Day Wanes:
  Time for a Tiger
  The Enemy in the Blanket
  Beds in the East
The Right to an Answer
The Doctor is Sick
The Worm and the Ring
Devil of a State
One Hand Clapping
A Clockwork Orange
The Wanting Seed
Honey for the Bears
Inside Mr Enderby
Nothing like the Sun: A Story
  of Shakespeare's Love-Life
The Eve of Saint Venus
A Vision of Battlements
Tremor of Intent
Enderby Outside
MF
Napoleon Symphony
The Clockwork Testament; or,
  Enderby's End
Beard's Roman Women
Abba Abba
Man of Nazareth
1985
Earthly Powers

for children

A Long Trip to Teatime
The Land Where the
  Ice Cream Grows

verse

Moses

non-fiction

English Literature: A Survey
  for Students
They Wrote in English
Language Made Plain
Here Comes Everybody: An
  Introduction to James Joyce for the
  Ordinary Reader
The Novel Now: A Student's Guide
  to Contemporary Fiction
Urgent Copy: Literary Studies
Shakespeare
Joysprick: An Introduction to
  the Language of James Joyce
New York
Hemingway and His World
On Going to Bed

translator

The New Aristocrats (with Llewela
  Burgess)
The Olive Trees of Justice (with
  Llewela Burgess)
The Man Who Robbed Poor Boxes
Cyrano de Bergerac
Oedipus the King

editor

The Grand Tour
Coaching Days of England
A Shorter Finnegans Wake

This Man and Music

Anthony Burgess

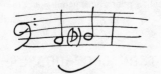

McGraw-Hill Book Company
New York • St. Louis • Toronto
Mexico • Hamburg • San Francisco

1 2 3 4 5 6 7 8 9 F G R F G R 8 7 6 5 4 3

ISBN 0-07-008964-7

Library of Congress Cataloging in Publication Data

Burgess, Anthony, 1917-
This man and music.

1. Burgess, Anthony, 1917-   . 2. Music and
literature.   3. Music—Philosophy and aesthetics.
I. Title.
ML80.B82B9 1983   823'.914   83-9876
ISBN 0-07-008964-7

To

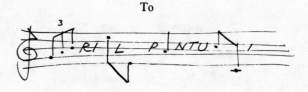

ACKNOWLEDGEMENTS

The author and the publisher wish to thank the following for permission to reproduce quotations in the text of *This Man and Music*:

Chappell Music Limited, for 'Yet' from *A Little Night Music*, words and music by Stephen Sondheim, © Rilting Music and Revelation Music Publishing Corporation; 'Why Can't The English' and 'A Hymn to Him' from *My Fair Lady*, music by Frederick Lowe, words by Alan Lerner, © 1956 Lerner and Lowe, original publisher Chappell & Co. Inc. by arrangement with Laval Corp.; 'Mountain Greenery' from *The Garrick Gaities*, music by Richard Rodgers, words by Lorenz Hart, © 1926 Harms Inc.; 'Thou Swell' from *A Connecticut Yankee*, music by Richard Rodgers, words by Lorenz Hart, © 1927 Harms Inc.

Chappell Morris Limited for 'Put On A Happy Face' from *Bye Bye Birdie*, music by Charles Strouse, words by Lee Adams, © 1960 Strouse and Adams, original publisher Edwin H. Morris & Co. Inc.

Famous Chappell for 'Love Is Just Around The Corner' from the film *Here Is My Heart*, words and music by Lewis Gensler and Leo Robin, © 1934 Paramount Music Corp.

Campbell Connelly Group for 'Monotonous', lyrics by June Carroll; 'Mamma, I Wanna Make Rhythm', by Jerome Jerome, Richard Byron and Walter Kent.

Francis Day and Hunter for 'Manhattan', by Richard Rodgers and Lorenz Hart, © 1925 E. B. Marks Music Corp. (USA).

The Bodley Head for extracts from *Ulysses*, by James Joyce.

David Higham Associates Limited for 'Sir Beelzebub' from *Collected Poems*, by Edith Sitwell, published by Macmillan.

Contents

Foreword

Some day, I hope, there will be a really substantial book about the relationship between the art of words and the art of sound, though I doubt if I, whose approach to both arts has always been highly empirical, will ever be sufficiently qualified to write it. Such a book ought to be addressed to the ordinary reader and listener, who have, or has, a right to intelligible answers to questions about beauty and meaning, as also to the resolution of confusion about the literary intentions of music and the musical intentions of literature. Works which probe the semiotics or the psychology of music are not, as a rule, helpful even to musicians, and they rarely enter into that 'philosophical' realm where the art is shown in relation to life. What I have done here is to examine in plain language those areas where music and literature undoubtedly meet – uncomplicated regions where musical rhythm elucidates prosody or symphonic structure has something to say to the reader of fiction. I have also tentatively approached the damnable problem of the meaning of music, but in no hope of a satisfactory solution. I address the common reader, though I fear I have been forced to baffle him occasionally by using technical terms: it is not always easy to avoid them, and it is perhaps as dishonest to avoid talk of the dominant seventh as it is, when discussing the internal combustion engine, to pretend a carburettor can be called by another name. Where passages of musical notation appear in the book (there are not many), the non-reading reader is invited to get help from a musical friend; alternatively he may ignore such passages.

I have practised all my life the arts of literary and musical composition – the latter chiefly as an amateur, since economic need has forced me to spend most of my time producing fiction and literary journalism. I set down these highly personal meditations in order to clarify my own perceptions of the two arts, but have to confess that the clarification seems to me to be of the most elementary kind. Because we think in words, the semantics of literature does not offer insuperable problems, though none of us understands the nature of a poem, play or novel as well as he thinks. With music the whole question of understanding fails for lack of the right expository language: we fall back, as in wine-tasting, on metaphor and analogy. And yet we hear music every day of our lives, and sometimes every hour of every day, without raising the question of its intelligibility. The question has to be raised sometimes, nevertheless: we have to examine our aesthetic sensibilities as we have to examine our consciences. An unambitious book of this kind, nibbling at kindred though easier questions, may help to chop down some of the obfuscatory vegetation which has grown into a grove and, indeed, a Grove.

Baker Street, 1982

I
'Biographia Musicalis'

I was born in Manchester in early 1917 while my father was
serving in the Pay Corps. When I was eighteen months old he
came home on leave one day from his barracks in Preston to find
my mother and six-year-old sister dead from Spanish influenza
and myself chuckling away in my cot. My mother had been a
singer and dancer in the old music halls: as I never knew her, it
has always been easy to make a myth of her, exaggerating both
her talent and her beauty. She had been professionally known as
the Beautiful Belle Burgess, a pleonastic title. My father had first
met her when sitting in in a pit band for the regular pianist, who
was down with alcoholic gastritis. My father, though he played
the piano very adequately and, like most British musicians, was
a superb sight-reader, was never himself a professional. He had
been trained in book-keeping and became chief cashier of Swift's
Beef Market, reserving pianism for his spare time. Three years
or so after my mother's death he married an Irish widow who
kept a very large public house in North Manchester. This was
the great Golden Eagle of Miles Platting, with its innumerable
snugs and bars and its three singing rooms with a piano in each.
In the evenings my father played one of these pianos, accompanying small professional comedians and ballad-singers and the
better kind of amateurs. He sat in also for cinema pianists down
with alcoholic gastritis.

There was thus in my early life an ancestral memory of the
music hall and the actuality of much popular music. The north-
west of England, as is well known, has contributed a great deal
to the demotic British stage and to the music associated with it,
and this may have something to do with the religious traditions

of the region. Many Lancashire families resisted, as did mine, the Protestant Reformation and were thus, until the Catholic Emancipation Act of 1829, cut off from the social and economic advancement that depended on higher education. The universities were closed to English Catholics, and the only 'profession' traditionally open to talent was the the popular stage. The term itself, especially when exalted to '*the* profession', is self-defensive or, if you wish, defiant. It is a bark from the underdog.

Dublin is not far from Liverpool, and Catholic Lancashire has allowed the indigenous forms of its culture to be influenced, and sometimes swamped, by Ireland. More than that, Anglo-Saxon Catholic blood has been much mixed with Irish, and the situation of my own family was typical. My father's father was half-Irish, and he married a peasant woman from Tipperary named Mary Ann Finnegan. My mother's family was Scotticized Irish and had a Jacobite martyr to match the Elizabethan martyr of which my father's family sometimes boasted. What, you will want to know, has all this to do with music? Only that the songs of my boyhood were as much Irish as English, with the occasional cry of Jacobite rage from north of the border and our prized special tribute from Bonny Prince Charlie in the song 'Farewell, Manchester'. That I never knew *Hymns Ancient and Modern* but did know Gregorian chant. That the highest secular music that came into my early life was what had been popular in James Joyce's Dublin – opera of the order of *Martha* and *The Bohemian Girl*.

When, as a boy, I was not living above a pub I was living above an off-licence liquor store or a tobacconist's shop. We were, as befitted our deprived Catholic tradition, always in the trades that promote conviviality – smoking and drinking: we never baked bread or butchered cattle. Above the shop or pub there was a sitting room, and in this there was always a piano. There was a piano stool that opened to disclose a music library, and this library consisted mostly of tattered sheet music – 'Come Back to Erin, Mavourneen, Mavourneen'; 'Finnegan's Ball'; 'Here's Another One Off to America'; a selection from George M. Cohan's *Little Nelly Kelly*; 'Smilin' Through'; 'My Little Grey Home in the West'; 'Love's Old Sweet Song'. There was a volume coverless and with broken stitching called *Gems of Old Ireland*. There were also the fortnightly parts of a series named

Music Masterpieces, with simple piano selections from *La Bohème* and *Madame Butterfly* and the Grand March from *Tannhäuser*, as well as 'Less than the Dust' and 'Pale Hands I Loved' from the *Indian Love Lyrics* and songs from musical comedies long forgotten. 'Leander', for instance, from *Leander*:

> On our verander
> Out in far Ugander
> Our lives hand in hand-er
> We'll squannder
> In song.

And a chorus from Lionel Monckton's *The Dairy Maid*:

> Maidenly mixtures of youth and utility,
> Dainty as Dresden, domestic as Delph,
> Doing our duties with calm capability,
> Airy and cool as the dairy itself.

More distinguished, a positive *book* in four volumes, was *The Music Lover's Portfolio*, which was too big for the music stool so rested on top of the piano. This contained its share of popular ballads – like 'The Old Sun Dial in My Garden' (the vocal line stressed *dial* very heavily) and 'There is No Death' – but also a piano reduction of Tchaikovsky's Fifth Symphony and of the Prelude to Act III of *Lohengrin*. It was only when (I will come to this later) I had myself learned to make sense of the keyboard that these 'classics' were heard in our sitting room, causing the customers below to complain. They were considered by my stepmother and her family to be far above our station.

On Christmas night there was always a great family party, and my father hammered away and my stepmother's younger daughter more genteelly tinkled. The sitting room was crammed with relatives of both families – my father's plumber brothers and their wives and children, the priests and greengrocers of the Manchester Dwyers into which my stepmother had previously married. Everybody had his or her own song (I remember a priest singing 'Be Mine, My Marguerite'), and even my stepmother, nesciently putting right Buck Mulligan in *Ulysses*, gave out with

> We'll be merry
> Drinking whisky, wine and sherry,

All be merry
On Coronation Day.

I sang a sea-shanty called 'The Golden Vanity', and I sang it
badly. I had no voice. I had no musical talent. It was recognized
as a matter for deep shame that I had been given a chance to
join the sopranos of the choir of the Holy Name, where Father
Bernard Vaughan had regularly preached (Pilate, wy don't you
old back that owlin mob?), and had flunked the voice test. I had
failed to inherit either a good ear or a musical interest.

I did not, in fact, care at all about music. When I was seven,
I was made to go to Mr Bradshaw's School of Music on Moss
Lane East, Moss Side, Manchester, there to be given violin
lessons. It was, as we all see now, an admirable aspect of the old
lower middle class life that everybody should be able to make
his own music. I could not carry a tune and I used the piano
only as a percussion instrument for expressing tantrums, so there
was only the violin left. The violin was a small instrument and
hence fairly cheap. Mr Bradshaw was very eager to sell violins.
I treated my violin badly. I chipped the varnish and broke one
of the pegs. My bow was a disgrace, unresined and filthy and so
slack that I could have played baroque four-part harmony with
it if I had wanted to or had known what it was. Mr Bradshaw's
school was a private establishment dependent on fees, so I was
not thrown out of it. Still, it was known that I was hopeless.
There was a little piece called 'Andante' which was nothing more
than an alternation in crotchets, whatever those were, of the
open strings D and A, and I could not even play that. The final
piece in Volume I of the violin tutor we used was called 'Maiden,
why criest thou?' It was just three or four notes on the E string,
and I would pretend to be playing it with the rest of the class
while Mr Bradshaw accompanied us on his trap drums. I became
expert in pretence, even to the use of vibrato, but I never learned
to sound a note, stopped or open, that was not, as they say,
vaccicidal.

Finally I pretended to go to my lessons but actually nursed
my violin case for an hour in nearby Whitworth Park. The bills
came punctually in and were paid. My truancy was discovered
by a shop-customer. There was a terrible row. I should have

been put off music for ever, especially the violin. The curious
thing is that I was to acquire a kind of theoretical or ghost
proficiency in the instrument. I was to learn, without ever physically touching a violin again, a kind of sympathy for violinists
and even a desire to help, though at a distance, aspirants to
competence on it. In 1947 I wrote violin exercises, with piano
accompaniment, designed to make melodic sense of open-string
playing and the addition of successive semitones to the open
string to the limit of the first position. Here was a waltz:

And here was a kind of barcarolle:

And here what I called a National Song:

I called the compilation *The Young Fiddler's Tunebook* and sent
it to Messrs Curwen, the music publishers. They liked the idea,
they said, but they could not as yet hold out hope of publication
because of the post-war paper shortage. It didn't matter. The
young fiddler I had written for was my long-dead self.

A year or two ago I composed a virtuoso concerto for Yehudi Menuhin. He finds the work wholly playable, he says, but he cannot as yet hold out hope of performance. It doesn't matter. I was merely keeping a kind of ghost faith with the young fiddler grown mature and brilliant. I do not think I have ever written an unplayable string part. String players, indeed, tell me my parts are not adventurous enough: I keep close to the open strings and still seem to have a very young fiddler in mind. But all this is anticipation. I have to get back to the child who failed in music but didn't care a fig for his failure.

Before the Second World War Manchester had a fine orchestra. It still does, but the Hallé is not as great as it was under Hamilton Harty. When the BBC Symphony Orchestra was formed, the Corporation, rich in those days, lured away most of the Hallé's section leaders for salaries Manchester could not afford to pay, prompting Hamilton Harty to curse the BBC publicly and cry out in the press against 'amiable bandits'. My father would occasionally go to a Hallé concert, especially if bleeding chunks of Wagner were being retailed or there was Strauss's *Don Juan* or Rimsky-Korsakov's *Scheherezade*. Some of the players were his drinking friends, especially Charlie Collier, the first harpist. My father gave me another chance to be wooed by music. He took me, at the age of twelve, to a Wagner concert. We had to stand in the promenade area at the rear of the Free Trade Hall, whose heating grilles gave off a strange musty smell which I was to meet again in Fraser and Neave's tonic water in Singapore. I liked the timpani in the *Mastersingers* Overture and did not object to the Venusberg Music from *Tannhäuser*. But on the whole I was bored and my legs grew tired. I did not wish to go to another Hallé concert.

But a few days later I found a tune in my head and, having croaked it to him, asked my father what it was. It was, he told me, the second subject or aspiring tune of the *Rienzi* Overture. I was surprised that I had remembered it, and so was he. It seemed to me wrong that a theme from a piece of serious music should be as memorable as the dance tunes I was beginning to listen to on the radio. In our combined dining-and-sitting room behind the shop (the off-licence liquor store on the corner of Moss Lane East and Lincroft Street in Moss Side, eventually to become a West Indian shebeen) we had a five-valve radio from which I took in all the trash I could. But I was not permitted to listen to late-night dance music on it. Accordingly, up in my attic bedroom, I assembled a radio of my own, with coil, variable condensor, earphones, cat's whisker, and carborundum pyrites. There has, I swear, never been radio sound to touch that which came from a crystal set. One Saturday afternoon, when I should have been on the soccer field, I scratched my crystal with the cat's whisker, searching for Jack Payne and his BBC Dance Orchestra, when I got instead a kind of listening silence with coughs in it, and then a quite incredible flute solo, sinuous, exotic, erotic. I was spellbound. The velvet strings, the skirling clarinets, the harps, the muted horns, the antique cymbals, the flute, above all the flute. Eight minutes after that opening flute theme the announcer told me I had been listening to Claude Debussy's *L'Après-midi d'un Faune*.

There is, for everybody, a first time. A psychedelic moment, as they say or used to say nowadays, an instant of recognition of verbally inexpressible spiritual realities, a meaning for the term *beauty*. It was necessary for me to hear that work of Debussy's again, but there was no question of insisting that my family buy a wind-up gramophone and a plum-labelled twelve-inch shellac plate with the faun's music incised on its two sides. Subscribe to the *Radio Times* (a bulky cultural journal in those days), keep an eye on the Hallé posters. But I also had a desire which showed me to be a genuine musician in obscure latency, not a mere pounder or squawker or scraper: I wanted to know what that music *looked like*, I sensed that its eternal reality, as opposed to the evanescent reality of performance, lay in printed symbols. I would have to learn to read music, something that trap-drumming Mr Bradshaw had failed to make me enthusiastic to do. How did I start?

My father was unhelpful. I had had my chance and failed. He would not even indicate the double location of middle C – the note on the keyboard, the sign on the stave. Besides, he was beginning to give less of his spare time to his family, devoted to draught Bass and his boozing friends. But I found that middle C without his help on the untuned upright in the long cold sitting room above the liquor store. It lies to the left of the female

half of the lock of the piano. It is on a leger line below the treble
stave or above the bass stave. It is in the dead middle of the
eleven-line great stave. Find middle C and you have found everything. I remembered from the abortive fiddling days that the
spaces of the treble stave spelt FACE and the lines EGBDF,
standing for 'Every good boy deserves fivepence' (note the
Manchester commercial touch; all that good boys get further
south is favour). I made up my own mnemonics for the bass
stave. In the spaces the gambler draws an ACE – Gee! The lines
say: Go Bring Dad Five Apples.

As for the duration signals – semibreve, minim, crotchet,
quaver, and the half-lengthening dots – this was a simple matter
of counting beats: ONE (two three four); ONE (two) THREE (four);
one two three four; one and two three and four. A sharp (the
symbol had eight sharp points) meant playing the nearest black
key to the right; the other symbol had to be a flat (nearest black
key to the left). All this was easier than learning French. What
was needed, as with French, was practice. I found at the bottom
of the piano seat a yellowed torn sheaf of two-part pieces by
Handel. I learned them painfully, note by note. By my fifteenth
birthday I was able to make an attempt at any keyboard piece
that did not have rapid runs in it. I never attempted the dull
Parnassian climb of agile major and minor scales, as decreed by
Czerny. Big chords were and still are my line. I taught myself to
play the piano but not to become a pianist. I wanted to become
a composer, like Debussy. My family was unsympathetic. There
was no money in it.

I was listening to more 'serious' music now on my bedroom
crystal receiver. Not piano recitals, not string quartets; I wanted
the full orchestra, whose sonorities I tried to evoke at the keyboard. Music before Wagner had little appeal: it was orchestrally
naive, the trumpets and horns were mere bugles, the strings did
not divide into a velvet shimmer, there was no bass clarinet or
cor anglais or percussion section. Modernity began for me with
L'Après-midi d'un Faune, whose miniature score I bought with
a fifteenth-birthday gift of five shillings – a lot of money in those
days for twenty-eight pages of bad Durand & Cie engraving. I
tried to read the scores of Schönberg's *Pierrot Lunaire* and
Stravinsky's *Le Sacre du Printemps* in the Manchester Central

Library. I was acquiring an anecdotal musical general knowledge
from the excellent old *Radio Times*. This taught me, for instance,
that Cosima and von Bülow laid on a charade for Wagner, weary
with *Parsifal*, and the word first anatomized then presented
whole was *Tarlatane* (a cushion representing a Tartar is chopped
in half; the piano pretends to be an oboe and gives out the
tuning-up *la* or A; in Paris they say '*Wagner me tanne aux airs*',
punning on *Tannhäuser*). I learned that Debussy himself had
welcomed Sousa's band to Paris and described in the musical
press the great Philip Sousa catching butterflies fluttering from
the bass tuba. I learned a lot of things, mostly perhaps useless.

And yet this extracurricular concern with music, a subject not
taught at my school, gave me a smattering of European culture
not unhelpful in class and term examinations. Nobody except
me could translate *noisette*; I could assert that *tanner* meant to
bore. I could superficially compare Goethe's *Faust*, thanks to
Gounod and Berlioz, with Marlowe's *Dr Faustus*, which was a
set book. I had picked up a little Italian and German and had
even tried to translate the text of *Pierrot Lunaire* into English. I
could painfully decipher Cyrillic script, for this was to be found
at the head of the score of *Le Sacre*. *Carmen* led me to Merimée
and *La Bohème* to Mürger. When, in the English literature
paper of the School Certificate examination, I was asked to dif-
ferentiate stylistically between Tennyson's *Lotus-Eaters* and
Ulysses, I said that the first had the voluptuousness of the Venusberg Music and the second the austerity of Sibelius's Seventh
Symphony. This did me no good: I should have said that the
first rhymed and the second didn't.

Meanwhile the spare-time occupation of trying to turn myself
into a composer raised, in embryo, the problems which still
oppress genuine students of the art in genuine academies. (I was
aware, and still am, that there is a lack of genuineness about the
self-taught.) I mean: what musical language to compose in?
There were many available in the 1930s, and they were all of
their age – that is to say, they would have been gibberish to
Beethoven and even to Wagner. There were all the dialects of
Stravinsky, from *Le Sacre* (only twenty years old when I began
to draw notes on paper) to the time-travelling which, in his *Music
Ho!*, Constant Lambert deplored. There was the full-blown

atonal school of Vienna, whose tricks even the tin-eared could learn. Honneger and Mossolov imitated machines. My own country had produced a chordal polyphony (as in Ralph Vaughan Williams's Pastoral Symphony), very diatonic and yielding to folkiness. The linguistic issue had not yet been further complicated by the Moog synthesizer, the timed silences of John Cage, or the aleatory principle, but there was Babel enough. There was also a profound contradiction between what one heard (freely indulged consecutive triads, for instance, even as early as Elgar) and what one had to learn (consecutive fifths an abomination, the false relations praised in William Walton condemned in the textbooks). Textbooks froze harmony, counterpoint and orchestration into postures that Beethoven and even Haydn rejected.

Still, the textbooks had to be studied – the Novello primers with the stylized lute and stars of celestial attainment on the cover. I doggedly trod through Stainer on harmony (Kitson was far better: Kitson admitted the existence of secondary sevenths), Higgs on fugue, Prout on the pre-Romantic orchestra. At least one learned the terms, found out that there was a good acoustic reason for not doubling the mediant, saw the stylistic point of contrary motion. But it was a long way away from real music, whether discoursed by Adrian Boult and the BBC Symphony Orchestra or Henry Hall and the BBC Dance Orchestra.

I did not, as I might have done, now start to despise the popular music of the time. I played it on the piano, and it did me good with the girls. Its harmonies were a long way from Stainer: you had to add a sixth and even a second to a common chord; you played tenths in the bass; you harmonized the dominant with, first, a seventh or ninth on the supertonic, and then, for an effect of post-*Tristan* intensity, a ninth on the flattened supertonic. The pert or swoony derivative of jazz had its own rules. It had its social function; it was not to be sneered at, despite the gibe of 'masturbatory' from the *Musical Times*. And even the *Musical Times* had to admit the successful absorption of jazz tricks by Ravel and Stravinsky.

I was growing up, shaving, in the sixth form. It was time to take the Higher School Certificate. I wished to offer music as one of my three advanced-level subjects. There was perturbation and opposition. My school had no great academic reputation; I was not unbright; with English, Latin and Modern History I had the chance of gaining three Ds or distinctions to the glory of the school. I insisted on offering music, not history. But, they said, we know nothing at all of your ability in the subject; we have not taught it you; we are in the dark. Deaf, you mean, I said, you have been criminally deaf. I demanded that I offer music, and they (headmaster and prefect of studies) yielded with an ill grace.

There were two three-hour papers and a viva voce. The first paper examined one's knowledge of three set works – Haydn's *Creation*, Schubert's 'Trout' Quintet and Brahms's Second Symphony. The second paper asked for the reduction of a passage of full score to two staves for the piano, the musical setting of a poem (this year it was a sonnet by Felicia Dorothea Hemans), and the four-part harmonization of a given theme. These tests were not difficult, but the oral examination was a nightmare, and there had been no means of preparing for it with regular drills. The examiner played on the piano first an unaccompanied melody in A major, highly chromatic, and I, and the other candidates, all girls, had to write it down. Then he played some four-part harmony in E flat, also to be transcribed, and finally a piece of two-part counterpoint. I did badly. I did well, however, when it came to answering questions about variation form and string harmonics. Then I was asked what percussion instruments Brahms had used in his symphonies. Timpani only, I replied, except in the third movement of the Fourth, where he introduces a triangle. I got through. I gained a distinction in music, and the school was proud of me, meaning proud of letting me have my own way.

My formal education had now, according to my father, ceased. I must now get a job. The year was 1935, and there were not many jobs around. I said I was willing to play the piano in a pub, but my father, rightly, dismissed this as a mere beer-soaked hobby. Finally he announced that, while still looking for a job, I was to help with the parcelling and delivery of orders for the wholesale tobacco store my stepmother now owned and he ran, and I was, in the evenings, to prepare with a correspondence school for next year's public examination for the Department of Customs and Excise. This was a highly competitive examination:

out of an expected thousand candidates only five would be selected. I did not stand a chance, and I knew it. Chemistry was an essential subject, and it had ceased to be taught in my school after the blowing-up by a disaffected South American pupil of the chemistry laboratory. I had to learn it from a book and set up experiments in the lab of my mind. There was also geography, and the textbook was too ill-written to take seriously. I was now not only musically knowledgeable but also well read in literature. I knew much of Gerard Manley Hopkins by heart and had copied out, in a very neat hand, the whole of Eliot's *The Waste Land* from the public library collection of his verse (a very small collection then; it was not to be much greater later). My former history master had smuggled in the Odyssey Press edition of *Ulysses* from Paris, and this too I had read. Despite this erudition I failed the literature paper of the Customs and Excise examining board. I was asked to discuss *Reynard the Fox*, *Greenmantle* and 'He Fell Among Thieves', but I did not know what these were.

I could have foretold the result from the beginning. The melancholy of a year's meaningless cramming was mitigated chiefly by music. I had by now composed a few brief things, including settings of the songs in *Sweeney Agonistes*, an orchestral dead march, a discordant trio for flute, oboe and bassoon, a prelude and fugue for the Holy Name organist (a post once held by the great Leslie Stuart, composer of *Floradora*), and a setting for male voices of the first dozen lines of Dryden's *Absalom and Achitophel*. I determined now to comfort my sad heart with the writing of a symphony.

It was in E major, which meant that in the first and fourth movements I had to draw four sharps for every non-transposing instrument at the beginning of every page (one sharp for clarinets in A but five sharps for cor anglais, which I now patriotically called the English horn) and this was far more tiring than setting down the notes. It was a melodious work – the melodic gift is a property of youth, like the lyric one – but melodies are not required in symphonies, except in the slow movement. What are needed are pregnant themes, as in Beethoven. Reluctantly I began to listen seriously to Beethoven and to try to play his damnable sonatas. I examined those twelve-stave orchestral scores which are so visually unexciting compared with *Iberia* or

Petrouchka. There was no doubt about it: old Ludwig knew how to make much of nothing. I was not mature enough to learn from the first movement of the 'Eroica', and the English symphony – Elgar, Vaughan Williams, the recently performed No. 1 in B flat minor of William Walton, a fellow-Lancastrian – was too much in my ears. My orchestration was Elgarian with Holstian condiments; from *The Planets* I stole a bass flute, six horns and four trumpets. The work was not, I knew, going to be performed any more than I was going to be elected to the Customs and Excise (a race of functionaries I hate but reluctantly admire), but I had to push on with it. Two hundred pages of full score, as thick as the manuscript of an 80,000-word novel. I learned, which was to quicken a growing stoicism, how physically taxing the composition of orchestral music is: sometimes four hours of scoring for one minute of sound. I learned, too, how thoroughly one has to imagine sonorities before setting down their bald symbols. And I realized how valueless the piano is as an aid to orchestral composition. A piano misleads, sets up the wrong sounds in one's head. I ceased to pity Beethoven, Smetana and Fauré for their deafness. Deafness was no great handicap: it shut in sonic realities against the intrusive and impertinent noises of the world.

What was the language of this symphony? A language altogether proper for a young man composing music in England in 1935. Diatonic, swift to modulate, inclined to the modal, Vaughan Williams harmonies, occasional tearing dissonances like someone farting at a teaparty, bland, meditative, with patches of vulgar triumph. Totally English music, hardly able to jump twenty-two miles into Europe. Here is a great mystery. Music is considered an international language, yet it tends to gross insularity. What makes English music English? An American conductor to whom I put the question said, cruelly: 'Too much organ voluntary in Lincoln Cathedral, too much coronation in Westminster Abbey, too much lark ascending, too much clodhopping on the fucking village green.' We all know where to find, egregiously, these properties – in Vaughan Williams's aspiring pentatonic violins, in the hushed treacle of *Gerontius*, in Holst's St Paul's Suite and the E flat tune (six soaring horns) of his 'Jupiter'. In the finale of my symphony six soaring horns give

out a mixolydian melody in four-square three-two time, full of
hope for the British future:

Nobilmente yet, God help us.

And yet there is Teutonic clodhopping enough in Beethoven
and Viennese *Schmalz* in Berg's Violin Concerto and travel-poster
Hispanicism in Manuel de Falla. These, however, somehow transcend their nationalism in a way that Elgar and Vaughan Williams do not. We can export Benjamin Britten because of a kind
of crabbed neutrality of language, but the 'international' (or
Mahlerian) neurosis of Elgar is hidden from the foreigner by the
coronation robes. This is, I need hardly say, all metaphorical
talk. Music is not about anything. Music has associations, but
no referents. *This* sounds like a *Ländler* we once heard in Graz,
and *that* effervesces with the very upper partials of the Changing
of the Guard, and here is a fragment of a cowman's ditty we
remember lugubriously floating over a June-soaked hedgerow.
All this is on the fringe of music, but it is more easily grasped
than the main fabric. My symphony in E major was, I think, all
fringes.

The headmaster of my school, an Irishman, a member of the
Order of St Francis Xavier, given to charm, drink, peasant
shrewdness, patrician irascibility, fantasy and solid sense, tele-
phoned my father to tell him that it was a crying shame that I
could not go to a university. A scholarship was out of the question, since only one state scholarship and one corporation scholarship were awarded annually in Manchester, and these regularly
went to the De Quincey type geniuses of Manchester Grammar
School; still, the fees were not excessive at the Victoria University
of Manchester, and I could live at home. My father surveyed my
jobless frustration, manifested in the piling up of the pages of
my symphony and occasional bouts of drunkenness, but thought
the university a hard remedy. Two things concurred to make
him change his mind: the maturing of an insurance policy which
my stepmother had slyly taken out on the odds of my living to

twenty, and my being dumped one night on the doormat by a policeman, out for the count, paralytically beered up, at the limit of frustration. Half the insurance money could go to my resumed education; in such spare time as I should have I could go on delivering tobacco orders to clubs, pubs, cinemas and the cut-price retailers of the slums. I should also have pocket money of two shillings every Monday morning.

Having obtained a distinction in music in the advanced level of the Higher School Certificate, I thought I was eligible to enrol in the music department of the university, but, to my great shock, I found I needed a minimal qualification in physics. The physics laboratory of my school had not been burnt down, and I had in fact studied the subject to Lower School Certificate level, but I failed the examination. My physics teacher had been a bad teacher, and he had left most of the instruction to one of my classmates, who had an eccentric talent for the subject. His name was Dowd, and he wore the black uniform of the British Fascist Party to school. (In another class there was an Italian named Adolfo Corradi, who wore the black uniform of the real Fascisti. He was eventually to marry one of my cousins.) I naturally refused to learn physics from Dowd, finding the arrangement irregular. So I had no physics with which to enter the university music department. I think physics was required so that students should know something about acoustics and the relation of tone to the expansion of metals. Manchester University was very physical in those days, even in the English department, which (having gained a distinction also in English literature) I entered as a *pis aller*.

For there we learned phonetics, which made some of the girls, who thought English was going to be all about the Beauty of the Imagery of the 'Ode to a Nightingale', cry. And if, through inattention, you found you were studying Old Icelandic, you had to go to Reykjavik to be examined in it. There was also practical criticism, with anonymous texts laid out on our desks like preserved frogs for anatomical probing. This too made some of the girls cry.

I went occasionally to sessions of the Choral Society, where Dr Proctor-Gregg cracked his baton on his desk like a pandybat and cried, 'Did no one teach you to count?', and then I was glad

I had not been acceptable to the music department. There is something childish about institutional or collective music, with bullying and corky choirmaster quips, public humiliation over wrong notes, shouting and hockey-mistress cajolery, facetiousness about chippy-choppy rhythms, 'Don't you eat ice cream?' if you fail to spot a Neapolitan sixth. I was, I began to see from consultations with bona fide students of the subject, better out of it, a free autodidact.

I still composed music, but other things got in the way – drama for the poor at the Ancoats Settlement, Joan Littlewood and her Living Newspapers, coeditorship of the university magazine, the writing of poems and short stories, beer, pub pianism (paid), rigorously sought and hardly achieved fornication. But I wrote the score for a projected and failed production of Flecker's *Hassan*, and was both Brecht and Weill in a number of cabaret presentations promoted at Students' Union dances by Klaus Pickard and Oskar Bünemann, research graduates in chemistry. I wrote the lyrics in English and they would translate them into German. German had a flavour of old Weimar chic and new Nazi brutality. It fascinated. Manchester was, in certain ways, closer then to Hamburg than to London. It had the atmosphere of a Hanseatic *Stadt*. It was full of German Jews long settled and became a refugee centre for the wretches of the new exodus. Our Hallé Orchestra played with German solidity and was happier with Strauss than Ravel. My own English department stressed the Teutonic ancestry of the language and seemed to offer the humanistic study of literature as a bait for catching potential scholars of Old Norse.

If university society wanted 'serious' music it went to the music department for it; from me it wanted Harold Arlen and Hoagy Carmichael. I wrote popular songs, had them performed, and tried to get them published. I was getting into the groove of demotic music, which, in a sense, meant getting ready for the war.

When war came, I volunteered for the Royal Army Medical Corps and trained at Newbattle Abbey, outside Edinburgh. I bashed the joanna in the NAAFI, volunteered for bagpipe instruction but soon gave it up (too much wind required on the march, the march doubly distressing on icy hills, the instrument itself a barbarous one), accompanied ballad-singers in 'Bless This House' and 'I'll Walk Beside You', was invited, with these same singers, into the decent middle-class homes of Eskbank to present a kind of tableau of young talent doomed to die, learned that piano players were a godsend to bored and weary troops.

I learned too that there was a great gulf fixed between the musical and the unmusical, and that most of the world was unmusical. Not, of course, in the sense of not wanting music, but rather in a diffused incapacity to understand the nature of music. Take the question of rhythm, for instance. On the march soldiers would sometimes be permitted to sing, and they always made the downbeat coincide with the crashing of the right boot. 'Yours till the stars lose their glory', much sung by Vera Lynn, was popular, but nobody had any notion of the number of beats covered by the second syllable of 'glory'. You could play a tune with outrageously wrong harmonies, and nobody would notice. Play drunk, and you were playing no worse than sober. At church parade the hymns were pitched too high for male voices, and non-singers were berated for not singing. No use explaining to the cursing corporal what was wrong. If a singer proposed singing something ribald, and you asked him what key he wanted, he would usually reply: 'We've only got one key to our 'ouse.' The ears of the great unwashed and washed alike were stuffed with fluff.

I was posted to a field ambulance in Northumberland and there became a brief hero. There was a dance, with girls from the village, and a band was expected from Morpeth. But the snow fell and the band could not get through. I played for four hours, I saved the evening. Gratitude, as it always is, was short-lived. 'Your fingernails,' said Lieutenant Somebody next morning, 'are, for a pianist, a disgrace.' This was HQ Company, formed pre-war as a territorial unit, all pals, homosexuality, family quarrels. I was not wanted. I formed a fife band of outsiders like myself. We learned to play the Corps march, a folksong called 'Pretty Joan', chosen by Vaughan Williams when he had briefly served as a medical orderly in the First World War. The words put to it by the troops were:

> We're browned off
> We're browned off
> We're always fucking well browned off.

There were complaints about our tempo on the march, so we too
became pettish and disbanded. A decent young intellectual in
the company, whom one rarely saw on parade, wanted a tune
for an anthem he had written for all three companies of the field
ambulance, so I provided it. But only he sang it:

> When we catch Hitler
> He'll be in an awful mess.
> We'll get a stretcher party
> To take him to the CRS.
> And the 123 Field Ambulance
> Will always do the trick:
> Around his balls a tourniquet,
> And a Thomas's on his prick.

A Thomas's being a Thomas's splint, which I could never learn
to assemble. I continued to try to please, however. I offered to
stand in for the sick bugler and, in the pre-reveille dark, con-
templated the mysteries of the harmonic series all wrapped in a
brass bent tube. I composed a special fall-in call for HQ Company, highly syncopated. Nothing would do. I was not one of
the pals. When the Entertainments Officer at Divisional Head-
quarters required a kind of musical director, I was very speedily
offered. I packed my kit and went.

The Entertainments Section was so called only on parade, a
periodic assembly which it managed badly and tried to shun. In
practice it was called the Jaypees Concert Party, after the initials
of the divisional general, John Priestland or somebody. It had
the following personnel: Lieutenant (formerly Captain) Bill El-
liott, 2nd Berks (with wife and dog), officer in charge; Sergeant
Harry Walkling, 1st Herts, tenor saxophonist; Corporal Pat
Glover, 2nd Berks, eccentric dancer and drag artist; Ted Norman, 2nd Berks, alto saxophonist and band leader; Bill Brian,
1st Herts, trumpet; Dick Nutting, Royal Artillery, double bass
and piano accordion; 'Styx' Williams, RASC, drummer and xy-
lophonist; Bill Clufton, RAOC, dancer; Douglas ('Charlie')
Close, RAMC, comedian; Paul ('Andy') Anderson, RAOC, light

comedian and monologuist; Ted Willis, 2nd Berks, officer's batman, electrician, casual comedian; Bob Morgan, RASC, violinist, Romano on the programme; Jack Varney, RASC, genuine lunatic, tenor. There was also a civilian girl dancer attached to the troupe, paid out of army funds, her name surviving as 'Babs'. There was now also myself. I was not welcomed.

The band resented the posting of their former pianist, a prodigy called Tommy, forgetting conveniently that he had himself requested return to his regiment to earn large money through playing at privately organized dances. They snarled at me as one raw and imposed. But, I soon discovered, everybody snarled at everyone – the singers and dancers at the band, the rhythm section of the band at the melody section, drummer at bassist, tenor at alto, trumpet at both and all. I soon settled into the snarling. My first job was to compose, words and music, and score a new opening chorus. The second half went like this:

> War, work and worry may shake you.
>   Still – don't back out.
> Here is a tonic to make you
>   Forget the blackout.
> So
> Just give us a hand now,
> We'll strike up the band now
> And let ourselves go –
> On with the show!

This was snarled at as unsingable and unplayable, but that was a mere ritual gesture. For the band was finding me useful in a way they had not expected. Genuine jazz records were now coming in from America, along with the GIs, and Bill Brian wanted trumpet solos notated, so he could learn them by heart. There was a record of Bing Crosby singing 'The Folks Who Live on the Hill', unavailable from the music publishers, and the whole band wanted a version of it. This I gave them, along with a transcription of 'If We Never Meet Again', which Bill had heard Louis Armstrong sing and play on a long-lost record and whose tune and riffs he remembered. Your bloody long-lost Tommy couldn't do that for you, I snarled at them. Tommy was all right, they snarled back. You leave fucking Tommy out of it.

So, on the whole, we all got on all right, dressed every evening
in black trousers, black bow tie and white bum-freezer, travelling
snarling in dirty trucks to entertain the units of the division
which, like all the home-based divisions, languished in the frost
of the Great Bore War. There was snarling for possession of the
body of Babs, but she kept that to herself. Some nights it was
the whole snarling troupe, other nights just the band, playing
for dances. We had all the latest dots coming in from Charing
Cross Road in conventional arrangements, but often I made fresh
and original ones, exploiting the lower notes of the trumpet for
a trombone effect, making the bass sound like a flute with bow
(previously cast into a cupboard) and harmonics, shoving deeply
resented Bob Morgan's violin close to a microphone to fake the
weight of a whole string section. And I orchestrated 'Macushla'
for Jack Varney the tenor (a dangerous man at full moon) and
'On the Track' for Styx's xylophone. I wrote a blues in waltz
time and a pseudo-symphonic arrangement of 'Darktown Strut-
ters' Ball'. And I learned to pound out, with bleeding little
fingers, the chords of 'I Came, I Saw, I Congaed' and 'I Know
Why' and 'Chattanooga Choochoo' and 'The Hutsut Song', and
all the rest of the offal so well remembered, the cheap perfumes
of privation, apathy, and possibly fear.

It was no bad thing for a would-be serious composer to learn
how to handle the resources of a six-part band. Stainer on harmony was useless here. All jazz chords add notes to the basic
triad, and what could be regarded as inessential decoration – like
the A glued to the triad C G E – becomes the heart of the chord.
Score the common chord of C for two saxophones, and you have
to have A C. Given a chord like C E G B flat D F sharp A to
reduce to three essential notes for two saxophones and one trumpet, D, F sharp and A would have to be chosen, leaving the
functional dominant seventh beneath them (C E G B flat) to the
piano. But the piano registers as a mere strumming, and the
double bass, plucking its four in a bar, does not provide what
Brahms would have regarded as a bass. In jazz harmony there is
no real bass, and you build your chord as a wasp builds its nest
– from the top down.

Jazz harmony is closer to Debussy than to Stainer or even
Kitson, but there is a kind of instinctual acoustic honesty about

it which owes nothing to impressionism. Western man has known, for a long time, that when you strike or rub a note on a string, you hear not just that note but, at least in theory, a whole aspiring cluster:

the note struck ⟶

The history of Western music has had much to do with the progressively making explicit of what nature leaves implicit. Harmony was with the Greeks no more than what was intended to be unison but, because some voices are higher than others, was in fact movement in octaves. Then the fifth was added and, in secular music, the third. The dominant seventh (e.g. the addition, over C G and E, of B flat) was a daring innovation during the Renaissance. With the dominant ninth (the addition of D) we have reached modernity. Jazz likes to sound the whole series, even in a final chord, because it is there in nature, not because it conveys a fancied emotional intensity. Indeed, the whole genre rejects emotional intensity: it is wholly anti-Wagnerian. It is not even happy in a minor key. Schönberg doubted whether the minor mode and its harmonies existed in nature, and jazz confirms the doubt. Given the chord of G minor – G B flat D – it invariably adds an E natural, thus half-cancelling the key signature and suggesting that we are hearing partials of the common chord of C major.

When, in obedience to the very different traditions of salon music, my little band had to accompany a soulful ballad, everything, however accurately played, sounded wrong. In jazz, saxophones give out neutral plastic and the trumpet quells its military brilliance; forced into the alien medium, made to speak of God or death or love, they become awkward and embarrassed. My musicians could meet 'serious music' on something like its own terms only in its baroque and impressionist phases. Bach is not soulful and he sustains his clockwork rhythms. I scored the Fugue in C minor from the first book of the *Forty-Eight* for this appropriate three-part combination (with extra parts for drum and double bass), and it worked, though it was not permitted to work in public, the world not yet being ready for the unlikely marriage. I fulfilled my boyhood ambition of wanting to have written *L'Après-midi d'un Faune* by adapting it for the group, but the rhythms of jazz took over and sweating privates and their doxies danced to it:

This life was, of course, all wrong for a soldier (black ties every evening, God help us), and my guilt was assuaged when I was promoted to sergeant and sent off for a serious prosecution of the war. Music, what there was of it for me, was mostly playing the mock-Rachmaninov of *The Warsaw Concerto*. But, posted to Gibraltar, I found Bill Brian the trumpeter and Harry Walkling the tenor saxophonist waiting for me in the Moorish Castle. Harry was now the drum major of the 1st Herts regimental band, a swanky baton-twirler at the Ceremony of the Keys, and Bill played a straight trumpet in it. But there was a dance band as well, and my 'special arrangements' were wanted. This time there was the glory of three trumpets, trombone, and four saxophonists (including E flat baritone): no difficulty now with setting out the full chord of the augmented thirteenth. There was also the military band itself, for which I learned how to compose marches, and a flute and drum band which played at the changing of the convent guard. I was back into music again. One hundred quires of thirty-stave manuscript paper were found gathering dust in a quartermaster's store on Line Wall Road. These had to be filled with dots.

On this Rock there were real, as opposed to army, musicians. There was a lance-corporal professor of harmony and a private former Director of Music for the county of Kent. These academics had to be shunned; I was not of their world. I was self-taught, could not play a scale without fumbling, did not know the Köchel numbers, was ignorant of some of the later quartets of Beethoven. I was a faker, a patcher, something of a showman. Asked to play Chopin on the piano of the YMCA, I would improvise the arpeggios, arguing to myself that the performing Chopin probably did not keep to the written notes. I liked to play jazz, which was all improvisation, and in those days there was no rapport between the jazzmen and the academics. I composed, but I did not let the professor of harmony see my compositions. He would point out elementary errors, the kind of thing a student of the Royal College of Music had pandybatted out of him in his first term. I was safer with the jazzmen, who did not give a damn about doubling the mediant. Still, I started a new symphony, in A minor, and I wrote a cello sonata for a shore-based petty officer who kept his instrument in an outsize sea chest. I wrote incidental music for *Tobias and the Angel* and *Winterset*, and the professor of harmony was not permitted to look over the shoulders of the performers. When the academics had been posted away from the Rock I felt freer and was more assertive. I ran the Gibraltar Music Society and gave lessons in orchestration to two pale leading aircraftmen. I organized musical appreciation evenings for the YMCA. I also approached the age of thirty and the end of the war with a very shaky sense of vocation. No one could earn his living as a composer, but what sort of a composer was I? An organist serving as a cipher clerk, a sort of composer himself, told me that composition was 'a nice hobby'. I, once destined to be a new Debussy, was pursuing a nice hobby.

The trouble was that destiny seemed to have an unwished-for vocation ready for slow delivery. At the university I had published verse in the union magazine and had won, with the late Harold Nicolson adjudicating, the large sum (it was large in those days) of £5 for the best short story of 1939. In Gibraltar I won the Governor's Poetry Prize. The unwanted literary gift, the enforced vocation, was cognate with the avocation I had to follow to earn a living. For I had a good degree in English language and literature, and I left the army with experience as an instructor. The chalky gown of a schoolmaster hung on a staffroom peg somewhere, waiting for me to indue it. But first I had to help train the new race of emergency teachers – ex-servicemen like myself who said they had a vocation to teach snotty kids in primary schools. I had specialized in Elizabethan drama and written a thesis on Christopher Marlowe. I had studied phonetics. I was deemed suitable for teaching drama and speech. At least I was in the realm of sound. I produced *Dr Faustus* and *Murder in the Cathedral* and *The Ascent of F6* and wrote the incidental music. It was still only a nice hobby. How did one persuade the great world outside to listen to one's notes? I sent the orchestral score of my Passacaglia to the BBC, and they sent it back. I was ready to assume the paranoia of the outsider. Surely students of the Royal Academy or Royal College of Music had their works performed in public, with BBC talent scouts listening from the shadows?

A nice hobby at the grammar school where I next taught, the headmaster and his family keen violinists, my Partita for Strings performed in Banbury Town Hall. The school was full of musical hobbyists: the chemistry master and my English-teaching colleague played the flute; the maths man had sung in Vaughan Williams's *Sea Symphony* and Holst's *Hymn of Jesus*; the French mistress was a superb pianist. At home in the evenings I toiled at a score too strenuous for a nice hobby, knowing that it would never be played. Or, if it should be played, where would it get me? I would have to pay for the copying of the parts and be content with one ill-rehearsed performance. How did professional composers live? In those days they didn't, unless they were Benjamin Britten. It was not the age of ample commissions and subventions. Composition was a nice hobby for even graduates of the RCM and RAM and the Guildhall School of Music. Weary of scoring and the high price of manuscript paper, one day I started to write a novel. It was published, and I now had another nice hobby. But, later, an invalid, informed that I probably had a year to live, jobless and pensionless, I had to turn the writing of fiction into a profession. I survived the terminal year, and so did the profession.

One thing I discovered when I had completed my third novel was that it was a temperamental necessity for me to cleanse my mind of verbal preoccupation by composing music. It no longer mattered whether the music would ever be heard: music was a kind of therapy. The mere physical act of ruling bar lines and setting down notes was a manual and visual relief from the long days at the typewriter. The struggle with words, their syntax and rhythms and referents, yielded to a concern with pure form. In terms of the music itself there was a salutary relaxation of tension. A professor of harmony could jab his bony finger on solecisms and infelicities, and I would not care. This is a purely therapeutic occupation. I am writing to please myself. This often turns out to be the best way of pleasing others.

In the early 1970s I produced, with great labour, a novel I propose to discuss in its formal aspects in a later chapter. It was entitled *Napoleon Symphony* and was an attempt to accommodate the facts of Bonaparte's career to the structure of Beethoven's 'Eroica'. An American professor of music read the book and wrote to me. He said that he had gained from the work an impression that I had studied music and perhaps composed it. Would I be willing to write a major piece for the university symphony orchestra, of which he was the regular conductor? God bless America, where chances are taken. I wrote a symphony (no. 3 in C), and it was performed and recorded. In middle age I heard myself for the first time discoursed by a hundred players. Any remaining tension about the adequacy of my composing technique was dissolved. There were faults, of course – woodwind balance sometimes ill-calculated, as in Beethoven, an excessive use of the side drum. But the symphony, whatever its aesthetic value, did not sound like the work of an autodidact. It had been composed – in Rome, Siena, American motels and airports – far away from a piano, and the inner ear was proved to have imagined the right tonalities.

I will not dwell on the irony of my securing a musical hearing through the practice of a different art: the lateral chance is not uncommon. I had already come to the professional theatre through the novel and, indeed, was for a year the literary adviser to the Tyrone Guthrie Theater in Minneapolis. I translated *Cyrano de Bergerac* and wrote incidental music for it. For the performing rights I was paid $500. The translation was a commercial success, and, ill-advisedly, it was turned into a Broadway musical. I wrote the lyrics but could not have done so without a musical background. The composer, a Welshman, had very doubtful notions of English prosody, and it turned out to be safer for him to write the tunes first and for me to fit words to them. These tunes were often delivered over the transatlantic telephone: key B flat, common time, anacrusis crotchet F, bar line, minim B flat, crotchet C – and so on. In contact with professional Broadway orchestrators, I grew aware of the tentativeness of their technique: they had to hear an arrangement played before they knew whether it was right, and often it was not right. Some of them could not read the tenor clef. I gained a casual confidence in my own musicality, something I had never had in Gibraltar.

The BBC, which once rejected me, has now played me. I plan big orchestral works for the future, but I am tied to the exercise of a literary profession. I am also, so far as the language of music is concerned, frozen in a remote time. Professional composers who found fame early are free to shed traditional weights – the whole great romantic orchestra, the resources of the diatonic. I have not finished with the orchestra of Strauss, and I am too old now ever to be ready for the aleatory or the electronic or the Cagean space of silence. I have had enough silence.

I have been trying, in this chapter, to sketch my credentials for the discussion of music and literature that I propose. I would like to particularize those credentials now, and at the same time indulge myself, by imagining that I have become a leaf of Grove. The Grove entries end with exhaustive lists of compositions. Here, as far as I can remember them, are mine. None of them is worthy of an opus number.

1934   Dead March for full orchestra
       'In pious times ere priestcraft did begin' for male
         voices
       Trio for flute, oboe and bassoon
       Albumblatt for small orchestra
1935   Songs for voices and piano from T. S. Eliot's *Sweeney*
         Agonistes
       Symphony (no. 1) in E major
1936   'Complaint, complaint I heard upon a day' (from Ezra
         Pound's *Cantos*) for SATB unaccompanied

String Quartet in G major

1937 Five twelve-tone studies for piano
'Nu we sculan herian' (Caedmon's Hymn) for male
voices
'Ic eom of Irelonde' for soprano and flageolet

1938 Sonatina in E flat for piano
Music for James Elroy Flecker's *Hassan*

1939 *Ich weiss es ist aus*: a group of cabaret songs (in
German)
'Blackout Blues': a group of cabaret songs in English
'Lines for an Old Man' (T. S. Eliot) for old man and
four instruments

1940 *Dr Faustus*: draft of a one-act opera

1941 Prelude and Fugue for organ: *Ipswich*
An Afternoon on the Phone: arrangement for six-piece
dance orchestra of Debussy's *L'Après-midi d'un Faune*
Hispanics: for violin and piano

1942 *Song of a Northern City* for piano
'Everyone suddenly burst out singing' (Siegfried
Sassoon) for voices and piano
Nelson: suite for piano (one eye, one arm, one ——)

1943 Sonata for piano in E major
Reveille Stomp for large dance orchestra
Purple and Gold: march for military band
Retreat music for flutes and drums
Symphony in A minor (abandoned)
Prelude and Fugue for organ: *Calpe*

1944 Sonata for cello and piano in G minor
Nocturne for piano
'Anthem for Doomed Youth' (Wilfred Owen) for chorus
and orchestra

1945 *Music for Hiroshima* for double string orchestra
Sonata for piano in E minor
Overture for large orchestra: *Gibraltar*

1946 Sinfonietta (abandoned)
Mass in G for chorus and orchestra (abandoned)
Spring Songs for soprano and orchestra: 'O western
wind'; 'The earth has cast her winter skin' (Charles
d'Orléans, trans. A. B.); 'Spring the sweet spring'

(Thomas Nashe)
'I sing of a maiden' (anon.) for voice and string quartet

1947 'This was real': a group of stage songs
'These things shall be': a celebration for Bedwellty
  Grammar School
'Inversnaid' (Gerard Manley Hopkins) for SATB
  unaccompanied
Three Shakespeare Songs for voice and piano:
  'Apemantus's Song'; 'Under the Greenwood Tree';
  'Come thou monarch of the vine'

1948 *Ludus Polytonalis* for chest of recorders
Incidental music for *Murder in the Cathedral* (small
  orchestra)
Incidental music for *The Ascent of F6* (small dance
  orchestra)
Moto Perpetuo, for large orchestra
Six Purcell Realizations

1949 Sonatina in G for piano
Sonata in C for piano
Sinfonietta for two pianos, whistlers, and percussion
  band

1950 Partita for string orchestra
Incidental music for *A Midsummer Night's Dream* (small
  orchestra)
Two wedding marches for organ

1951 Variations for double symphony orchestra (abandoned)
Guitar Sonata in E (unplayable)
Concerto for flute and strings

1952 *Terrible Crystal*: three Hopkins sonnets for baritone,
  chorus and orchestra

1953 Toccata and Fugue for cathedral organ

1954 *Ode*: celebration for the Malay College for boys' voices
  and piano

1955 *Kalau Tuan Mudek Ka-Ulu*: five Malay pantuns for
  soprano and native instruments

1956 Suite for small orchestra of Indians, Chinese and Malays

1957 *Sinfoni Malaya* for orchestra and brass band and shouts
  of 'Merdeka' ('Independence') from the audience

1958 *Pando*: march for a P & O orchestra

1959 Passacaglia and Bagatelle for piano
Suite for miniature organ
1960 Fantasia for two recorders and piano
1961 Twelve-tone polyrhythmics for piano
1968 Songs for *Will* (a film about Shakespeare projected but unrealized by Warner Bros.; music recorded)
1970 Incidental music for *Cyrano de Bergerac* (flute, clarinet, trumpet, cello, keyboard, percussion)
1971 *Southern City*: overture for large orchestra
Music for an Italian production of *The Entertainer* (John Osborne)
Roman Wall: march for orchestra
1972 Music for television series *Moses* (unacceptable to Sir Lew Grade)
Suite for piano duet
'Bethlehem Palmtrees' (Ezra Pound) for SATB
1973 *Faunal Noon* for harmonica and guitar
Sonatina in E minor for harmonica and guitar
1974 Symphony (no. 3) in C
1975 *The Eyes of New York*, music for a film (flute, clarinet, violin, cello and keyboard)
A Song for St Cecilia's Day (John Dryden) for chorus, organ and orchestra
1976 *The Brides of Enderby* (A. B.), a song cycle for soprano, flute, oboe, cello and keyboard
The Waste Land (T. S. Eliot), a melodrama for speaker and the above combination
1977 *Tommy Reilly's Maggot* for harmonica and piano
Suite for oboe
Nocturne for oboe
1978 Concertino for piano and orchestra
Concerto for piano and orchestra
1979 Concerto for violin and orchestra in D minor
Mr W. S., ballet suite for orchestra
1980 *The Blooms of Dublin*, an operetta based on James Joyce's *Ulysses*
Trotsky's in New York!, an off-Broadway musical
Nocturne and Chorale for four bassoons
Larry Adler's Maggots for harmonica and piano

1981   *A Glasgow Overture* for orchestra
       Preludio e Fuga per flauto, violino, chitarra e pianoforte
1982   *The Wreck of the Deutschland* (Hopkins) for
          baritone, chorus and orchestra
       Homage to Hans Keller for four tubas

2

A Matter of Time and Space

Music and literature have this in common – that the dimension
they work in is time. Having said that, I feel a twinge of dubiety
about literature, whose very name celebrates a kind of subordi-
nation of time to space, since 'letters' freeze the temporal flux of
speech into space-occupying symbols, and literature may be seen
as the artistic disposition of these symbols. To carve on a stone
slab some such line of verse as SVNT LACHRIMAE RERVM ET
MENTEM MORTALIA TANGVNT looks like the victory of
space over time: the flux, which carries everything away into
oblivion, has been arrested; an object occupying space, deep
incisions in a time-defying substance, proclaims the permanence
of letters, as opposed to the transience of speech. But to think
of literature in these terms is to confuse a reality with a mere
appearance. The reality of literature, as opposed to its appearance
in written or printed records, is the organization of speech
sounds, and this makes literature a temporal art, a twin of music.

On the other hand, if we take the reality of literature to reside
in a text, and not a performance, the art functions in the realm
of the eye, and not of the ear, and this draws literature away
from an art which, as is universally acknowledged, has no meaning except as an auditory experience. Shakespeare's plays are
intended for performance. The playwright himself, as far as we
know, had no interest in the printed text. If quartos of most of
the plays were published in his lifetime, this was to protect the
Lord Chamberlain's Men from the pirates. Shorthand writers
would take down garbled versions of the plays at whose performance they assisted, and then sell these imperfect transcriptions
to printers. If a 'bad' quarto of *Hamlet* circulated, the only thing

to do was to publish the true text in a 'good' quarto. This had nothing to do with Shakespeare's desire to be an Ovid or Virgil and transmit his works to posterity. The play to him was less a text than the sum of the performances of the play. But posterity itself has decided that Shakespeare was wrong, and that the reality of Shakespeare resides in a printed book. *Hamlet* is not the sum of its performances: it is an ideal and hence unrealizable performance. No acted version of *Hamlet* can be much more than a partial, and hence imperfect, interpretation of that supreme reality the text.

The text is clearly as much a spatial artefact as a painting, a sculpture, or a work of architecture. The eye can travel freely through it and over it. The printed words symbolize the temporal flux of speech, but they are an improvement on speech because visual solidity has replaced the transience of the auditory experience. In a knotty sentence of *The Winter's Tale*, unintelligible in performance, the elements can be disentangled by the eye, the statement broken up and then reassembled. This is as much a spatial process as the repairing of an automobile engine. But clearly Shakespeare never intended us to do this. The reality was the performance, and perhaps the unintelligibility was part of the artistic intention. We have come to regard the text as the great visual reality because we confuse letters as art with letters as information.

The legal document, the scientific textbook, the theological discourse with sidenotes and footnotes – these do not pretend to be literature in the sense that literature is an appeal to the imagination. In taking in printed information, we engage only the reason, and the reason is best satisfied if it can regard words as visual counters and not auditory complexes. If I read a line of poetry, I cannot be unaware of its auditory content: there will be a rhythm close to that of music, and there will be sonic organization in the verbal statement. But it will be possible to treat that line as a spatial entity, since my eye can travel over it as with a painting or a sculpture. In reading a formula like $a + a + a = 3a$ or 'If a body is immersed in water the loss of weight of the body is equal to the weight of the water displaced', the reason ignores the symbols as notations of speech sounds and concentrates on their semantic content. Works of literature, especially novels, are often treated in the same way. There is a confusion between the aesthetic and the didactic intentions, and we can end with the heresy that literature is a non-auditory art.

Now only to the highly ˚rarefied musician will the text of a sonata or a symphony be the primal reality. Ernest Newman, the eminent music critic and Wagner scholar, held that there was more true artistic joy in the silent reading of a score than in going to a concert. After all, Beethoven was deaf when he composed his greatest works, and who could deny the reality of the inner auditory experience of that towering genius? Newman seemed to regard Beethoven's deafness as a victory of the musical imagination over the crass imperfections of the physical ear: let us all be like Beethoven – i.e. deaf. But Beethoven would have given his eyes in order to have the use of his ears. The Newmanian heresy was, for a time, quite widely diffused. In the twenties there was one work that everybody knew but nobody had heard – Bernard van Dieren's *Chinese Symphony*. There was no great urgency in the arrangement of a concert performance: everybody who counted knew what the music sounded like. Cecil Gray, another eminent musicologist, composed an oratorio based on Flaubert's *La Tentation de Saint-Antoine*, which he had no intention of having realized in performance. The work was there in the text, not to be freed from it, and the musical reality could be shut away in a cupboard. It was commonly believed by Newman and others that Bach, having completed a complex work like the *Art of Fugue*, had no other desire than to shove it into a drawer and forget about it. Music was a kind of purgation on which the chain could be pulled.

There is, one must admit, a large temptation to regard a musical text as a spatial territory for free wandering. An orchestral score, especially a complex one like that of Stravinsky's *Le Sacre du Printemps*, looks like a non-representational work of visual art, and it invites slow and silent poring. We can take an orchestral sound to pieces and then put it back together again. We can analyse texture and appraise instrumental balance. But all this is ancillary to the auditory experience of performance: it is an aspect of learning about music and not listening to it. Any musical work is what Shakespeare presumably thought a play to be – the sum of all its performances. The play and the poem and the novel have come to be regarded as primarily visual realities because of the supreme physical advantages of a printed text – portability, porability, privacy. Though we can now carry around a miniature cassette-reader and a recording of *Hamlet*, it is unlikely that literature for the eye will easily let itself be superseded. But it is essential that we retain the notion of literature as meaningful sound, art working through time not space.

It is of course somewhat drastic to make a division of art into two distinct categories, these spatial, those temporal. Spatial art, such as painting, sculpture and architecture, cannot be divorced from time: there is no such thing as rigid instantaneity of perception of a picture, statue or cathedral. The eye has to travel over and through the parts which add up to the whole of the two-dimensional structure which is a landscape or portrait or non-representational pattern of line and colour. With the three-dimensional art of sculpture, the body as well as the eye must move to take in successively the various planes. The appraisal of architecture involves a kind of circular travel, within and without. But the time attached to the spatial arts is of a special kind when compared with the time through which music operates. Music begins at the beginning and goes straight through to the end; it is a fixed pattern of successions. The visual arts make time truckle to spatial form: time is rhapsodic, unpatterned. Time is an unfortunate necessity, not the stuff of the art itself.

The novel, though its material consists of events set in what J. E. McTaggart called the B series of time – binary, with things coming before and after each other, unlike the A series, which is ternary and has a past, a present and a future – reverses the situation which applies to the visual arts. When we read a novel we are aware of a three-dimensional solidity in our hands: we can travel through it as through a cathedral. We can anticipate the end, go back to clarify the identity of a character, go over the same paragraph more than once, and yet we know that this spatial motion is in the service of perceiving a segment of the B series of time. A lyric poem, especially if it is complex, admits a similar kind of spatial approach, and yet – though its content is probably concerned with a kind of eternal present (it does not present events as succession) – its form is as firmly temporal as that of a piece of music.

And yet the atomic materials of literature, the words out of which it is made, do not strike with a *significant* temporal force: we do not feel that words are made out of time, as dotted minims and groups of semiquavers are. A word is made out of a succession of phonemes, and succession means time, but the ear does not take in duration as the condition for uttering a word. This is partly because of the brevity of the duration involved – too short to be significant – and partly because words denote concepts or sense data, which the mind is schooled to regard as parachronic, or outside the flux of time. The difference between the vowel /ɪ/ as in *bid* and the vowel /iː/ as in *bead* is partly one of tongue position, partly one of duration – the second vowel takes twice as long to phonate as the first – but no untrained ear is aware of the time element involved. It took men a long time to learn how to represent words phonetically – that is, as a succession of sounds spatially notated; the Chinese and Japanese are still to arrive at the notion of an alphabet: an ideogram is an attempt at instantaneous symbolization of a syllable. Duration and succession are the subject matter of language, but words only begin to take on a temporal content when they are organized into patterns.

Musical notes are very different. In music we seem able to distinguish between two kinds of time, one internal, the other external, and neither has to do with the third kind – 'time' as a metrical signal, as three-four or four-four (which we can fancifully regard as the carving of the meat of duration into identical bite-size pieces). The duration of a piece of music is important in a way that the duration of performable literature (the play or the reading) is not. The performing time of a play is important for reasons which are mostly extrinsic – union overtime rules, the attention span of the audience. But the performing time of a piece of music, expressed in its tempo, seems to be an intimate part of its being. This tempo is important enough these days to be indicated with a metronomic mark – crotchet = 40 (forty beats to the minute) or minim = 100 (a hundred beats to the minute). It is not a matter of semantic importance how slowly or rapidly one word follows another, but the succession of musical notes is given affective significance by the speed of its utterance.

One thing we have to note about the comparative duration of

words and notes is the vastness of the spectrum of speed available to a musical statement and the narrowness of that in which verbal statements operate. We do not notice this in vocal music, where the setting will more or less accommodate itself to the tempo of the spoken word, but, when instruments play, the range of durations is spectacularly to be observed. The vocal organs are not so limited in speed of operation as we sometimes think: the vocal cords open and close, the tongue darts from phoneme to phoneme, the lips spread and round, all with great agility, but the vocal organs are no substitute for five fingers. Demisemi-quavers in fast tempo are idiomatic on the violin, but they are impossible to the voice. Wind instrumentalists require to take breath as do speakers or singers, but within the compass of a single inspiration many tied semibreves can be held or many tiny notes articulated. Yet the speed and slowness are not arbitrary or approximate, as in speech: they require exact designation. We can see now that to say that literature and music have the time element in common is to say very little.

The affective power of music, which depends so much on tempo, is one thing, but the structure of music is another. We have all had the experience of accidentally spinning a disc at the wrong speed. A record to be played at 33 r.p.m. changes its affective content when it is heard at 45 r.p.m. The instruments, in effect, are shrunken, losing in the lower range and gaining in the higher, but it is the change in tempo which disturbs. In the thirties, Benjamin Britten was commissioned by the Japanese to compose a symphony to celebrate the Emperor's jubilee. Britten misunderstood the commission and produced the *Sinfonia da Requiem*. The puzzled Japanese speeded up the tempo, but they could not make the music sound jubilant. The tempo, as much as the minor tonality, was built into the concept. And yet the structure, the inner time, the relationship of duration between note and note, was not changed. What we can call the work's absolute duration, the tempo heard by the composer and indi-cated in his score, was radically impaired in rehearsal (the work apparently did not reach performance, not in that place and not at that time), but relative durations were untouched. Of course, deliberate alteration of tempo can be an affective device, heard at its most comic in Saint-Saëns's *Carnaval des Animaux*, where

Offenbach's *Orpheus in the Underworld* cancan is slowed down drastically to represent the tortoise.

Time, then, the time of the metaphysician, becomes curiously transformed in music. The material of music is not, as it is in the narrative art of the epic or novel, the B series of McTaggart: there is no representation of successive human events. It seems that we are in the C series, where there is an order of perceptions, each of which is more inclusive than that which went before. (McTaggart argued that both the A and B series are illusory, and only the C system has true existence.) In music we perceive something, and then something else, and the second something is not perceived in isolation but in relation to the first something. When, in the recapitulation of a movement in sonata form, the exposition is made to return, this is not a reproduction of the past, since its content, though heard already, is radically changed by what has happened between its first and second statements. The total structure of a piece of music exists outside time in the sense that the only significant durations are relative: the timing of the whole work with a chronometer tells us nothing of the inner structure, though it will be highly relevant to the emotional effect the music has upon us. A dotted semibreve followed by a minim is the same structure as a dotted quaver followed by a semiquaver: it is all a matter of relative, not absolute, duration. So if Wagner's Overture to *Die Meistersinger*, whose playing time is normally ten minutes, is speeded up to five or slowed down to twenty, the structure is not impaired, the durative relations of the notes remain the same. But the meaning is different.

Is there a spatial element in music? Only in a metaphorical sense, and the manner of notating music is based on the metaphor: a score looks like a graph with temporal and spatial coordinates. The notes of the score travel from left to right in a representation of time; but notes are higher or lower than each other, and we seem to have entered a world of spatial relations. What makes one C differ from a C an octave higher is the rate of vibration of a string or membrane: time is there, rigorously measuring. But the terms used for describing the relationship between note and note derive from plane geometry, and the very notion of a scale derives from a *scala* or ladder. When notes are sounded simultaneously, as in a chord, it is not possible to speak of a simple temporal relation, and so the sister dimension has to be invoked. Moreover, there is an easy commerce between time and space in that a chord can also be an arpeggio – simultaneity becomes succession, yet there is total sonic identity in the structures. Add to the temporal (duration) and the spatial (pitch) such expressive devices as accent and sonic intensity, and you have the raw materials of music.

These raw materials are disposed in such a way as to produce structures which are aesthetically significant. Here we enter the dangerous world of artistic judgement, and we are easily lost. It is far easier to say why one line of poetry is better than another than to indulge in the relative evaluation of two melodies or themes. It is to be assumed that the lines

>   This my hand will rather
> The multitudinous seas incarnadine
> Making the green one red

are superior to

> Twinkle twinkle little star,
> How I wonder what you are,

and it is possible to say why. But a bad tune and a good tune are alike in manipulating pitch and duration, and one cannot call on such notions as adequacy of expression of emotion, unity of disparates, disposal of linguistic extremes and so on when comparing them. The following is universally taken for a good tune:

It is not, I think, the best tune in the world, not, for instance, as good as the Irish song 'The Lark in the Cleár Air', but such reasons as I can give for my judgement – monotony of rhythm, adherence to scalar pattern, limit of range – will not convince. Here is Beethoven at the height of his powers, setting Schiller's great ode, and here is exhibited his ultimate melodic mastery, etc., etc.

But what the melody, like any other melody, shows is the last and greatest element in the making of music – the building of forms, the creation of complex structures out of simple cells, the forging of significant unities out of repetition and contrast. From the simple structure of Beethoven's melody – A A B A – comes the whole of symphonic form. Duration and pitch, like the point-instants of the metaphysicians of time, combine to make a kind of world. I cannot enter Beethoven's mind, but I can, to some extent, enter my own, and I wish to examine now the way this mind works when it tries to create music.

3
Let's Write a Symphony

We know a good deal about the processes of literary composition as revealed by writers themselves, but, in respect of the details of the operation of their own craft, composers of music tend to a becoming dumbness: take my inexplicable magic and ask no questions. I propose now to describe, in such detail as I can remember, the composition of a work which was to give me what its auditors called an auditory breakthrough. I was requested by Professor James Dixon of the music department of the University of Iowa to furnish, if I could, a work of some substance for the university orchestra, and I chose to make this work a symphony.

But what is a symphony? Haydn, Mozart, Beethoven, Brahms and even Elgar knew, but we are no longer sure. Traditionally a symphony was a sonata for orchestra, in four movements – or separate sections preceded by silence – of differing tempi and character. The first movement was the weightiest, being in fast or moderately fast tempo and exhibiting the resources of sonata form. Sonata form is ternary, in the sense that the listener is aware of three main sections so closely stitched together that their seams do not show: the exposition, in which themes, or groups of themes, of a contrasting nature are presented (masculine–feminine; yin–yang; boisterous–lyrical); the development, in which the themes are involved in free fantasy; the recapitulation, in which the themes appear again as in the exposition, but with certain subtle modifications. The movement is rounded off with a tail or coda. In the symphonies of Beethoven, especially the 'Eroica', the coda is of such length as to constitute a section in itself, and the term quaternary seems more appropriate for the form of the movement.

An important aspect of sonata form, and one which we are – since the breakdown of the tonal system prophesied in Wagner's *Tristan* and fulfilled with Schönberg – no longer well able to appreciate, is the principle of the unity of key. A symphony usually announces its key in its very title, and the beginning of a classical symphony was often an emphatic statement of the key the first movement was in. If a symphony was in C, the first group of themes would be in that key, but the second group would be in a different key. The development, or free fantasia, would range over the spectrum of keys (twelve major and twelve minor being available), but the recapitulation would present the first and second groups of themes in the home key. The coda (as with Beethoven) might modulate, like a new development section, to remote keys, but the movement would always end with a reassertion of the key of the title.

The last movement would justify the title – Symphony in C or whatever – by being in the key of the first movement (or the tonic major, if the first movement was in a minor key: Beethoven's Fifth Symphony is in C minor, while the last movement is in C major), but the second movement would be free to choose a key different – though in the classical period not too remote – from the title key. The second movement was usually slow and meditative, but very occasionally – as in Beethoven's Ninth or Elgar's First – the slow movement was shunted to third place. The remaining movement was a minuet and trio in Haydn and Mozart, and invariably in the title key of the symphony. With Beethoven the minuet and trio were replaced by a scherzo and trio. With Brahms's first three symphonies we are given the gentler relief – between slow movement and strenuous finale – of a kind of lyrical intermezzo. Beethoven kept to the title key for his scherzi (except in the Seventh), but Brahms and his successors have felt free to get away from it.

Any composer proposing to write a symphony in the post-Brahmsian, or post-Elgarian or post-Mahlerian epoch is aware that the tradition stemming from Beethoven is no longer viable. With Sibelius the symphony ended as a terse one-movement form in which the aim was gradual transformation of themes, the development not being an incidental fantasy between two near-identical statements of a dual reality, but the essence of the work.

Thanks to Sibelius's innovations, and to the spread of the term symphonic to denote any kind of orchestral music not obviously balletic or lyrical, the very word symphony has become indefinable, except in historical terms.

And so, proposing to compose a symphony in four movements, with a loose allegiance, in the first and the last, to C as a tonal centre, I knew I was tackling an antique genre. I was, by the mere fact of restoring a traditional meaning to the word symphony, restricting my musical language to the pre-Schönbergian. I was opting for the diatonic, for key relationships which few contemporary auditors could find structurally significant, and for a sequence of contrasting tempi appropriate only to a dead culture. But I had two acts of homage to make, and I could only make them in diatonic language – one was to Shostakovich, who had recently died, and the other to a more remote master who is not even thought of in terms of music. I put aside expected rebukes for formal recidivism by reflecting that contemporary poets could choose to write in the sonnet form or Spenserian stanza: form mattered less than the validity of the personal statement.

I chose to write for an orchestra of traditional constitution: three flutes, the third doubling piccolo; two oboes, English horn; two clarinets in B flat; two bassoons and double bassoon; four horns in F; three trumpets in C; three trombones and bass tuba; chromatic kettledrums; cymbals, bass drum, side drum, gong, xylophone, glockenspiel, celesta; harp; strings. To these I added a piano and, in the last movement, a mandoline. In that same last movement a tenor and baritone would sing words expressive of my second act of homage.

A symphony was, before Sibelius's Seventh, expected to last at least thirty minutes. I foreheard mine as lasting something between thirty-five and forty, with this duration parcelled as follows: first movement, about twelve minutes; second (scherzo), five; slow movement, eight; finale, ten or more. Duration can be expressed in the number of bars envisaged. If the first movement is allegro vivo, and each bar (two-four or six-eight) is brief enough to last about a second, then about 700 bars, or perhaps sixty sides of score, will make up the required amount. As I planned a first movement which would have a slow introduction and a balancing slow coda, I felt that about 500 bars would provide the needed length. I had, at the outset, a dim image of the architecture of the movement expressed in a builder's estimate: 40 bars molto moderato as introduction; 400 bars allegro vivo (six-eight and sometimes nine-eight, dotted minim = metronome 60), divided into 150 bars of exposition, about the same of development, and 100, or possibly less, of recapitulation); coda adagio, about 60 bars.

This sounds both vague and cold-blooded. Music, surely, should flood from the heart, like Welsh oratory. Velvet sound, soaring or drooping themes, it should demand to be set down white-hot on paper, like the *Symphonie Fantastique* in the film of that name. But most composers will admit to the fact of the nebulous initial vision; the sense of a total shape and subordinate shapes within it; the occasional shadowy climax; oddities of texture; a flute solo not yet understood, let alone realized in sound; very little clarity of theme or development of theme. The vision of dry bones precedes the work of surveying; the rough scaffolding may come down any time: what the symphonist needs to start with is a kind of spatial image.

My first theme came not by concentration but, as is usual, distractedly, in a fit of absent-mindedness. It came in a kind of C minor, and I heard it on woodwind:

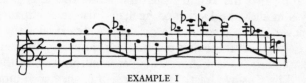

EXAMPLE I

It is not much of a tune; indeed, it is not a tune at all. It is just a humble theme, and it offers itself not for delectation but for development. Let us consider its possibilities. The first two bars came simultaneously in two forms – the first as notated here, the second with the second G missing in the second bar – a drop from the flat seventh to the supertonic and then on to the tonic:

EXAMPLE 2

This cadence suggests something once heard, or dreamed, vaguely Celtic, ancestral perhaps. The third bar is a leap in fourths followed by a held D flat, not to be found in the regular C minor scale but appearing in the chord of the Neapolitan sixth, which Cimarosa and other composers of Naples loved to use in a surprise cadence and which Beethoven employed in modulations. In the final bar we make our way back to where we started through a pair of fourths a tritone apart. These three segments of the theme can all be expressed chordally:

EXAMPLE 3

Chord (a) is a G minor triad in second inversion on a pedal C, indicating that the key in which the whole theme is pitched is really a mode – the Dorian or Aeolian – whose dominant chord will never have a B natural in it. This partly explains the ancestral, Celtic tone: those first two bars are closer to folk than to art music. Chord (b) is a chord of superposed fourths, of the kind beloved by Gustav Holst. The lower half of the chord moves up by a full tone, the top half down by a full tone, reaching a chord which seems to belong to two keys, since no one key could incorporate both D flat and D natural in its scale. If the chord is filled out, it will be seen to consist of the common chord of D flat and the common chord of G sounded together. The whole theme as good as enjoins the composer to make his harmonic language both cold and hot. To risk extravagance for a moment, there is an inhuman, almost Arctic quality about superposed fourths, and in chords made out of tritones we have the intrusion of the diabolic interval forbidden in the Middle Ages and still (consider the scherzo of Vaughan Williams's Sixth Symphony) loaded with connotations of the infernal.

Subsidiary themes began to trickle in after the decision to make Example 1 the main theme of the first movement. Example 4 seemed concerned with stressing the Dorian nature of Example 1, contradicting the A flat of its fifth bar:

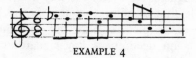

EXAMPLE 4

And Example 5 makes its first bar by pushing the first bar of Example 4 up one rung of the scale:

EXAMPLE 5

The first half of the second bar of Example 5 suggests that the two subsidiary themes can combine into a longer phrase:

EXAMPLE 6

This material, meagre as it seems, is quite enough for a first theme group. Armed with it, and trusting that the second group would work its way up from the unconscious while I concentrated on putting notes on paper, I felt confident enough to start ruling some bar lines. Professional composers compose in pencil, erasing as much as they write. I am foolhardy enough to set everything down in ink, evading errors as though I were performing a surgical operation. There is a purely visual and motor pleasure in inscribing, in indelible black, symbols which have their own calligraphic life. It is a return to the craft of the scribes, which I may not practise when producing books or essays. My need to

compose music after completing a lengthy typescript has a lot to
do with a nostalgia for pen and parchment. Scoring paper is not
like typing paper, thin and highly disposable stuff. It is large,
glossy, substantial. It deserves the respect of careful penmanship.

And so, on the first page, the space at the beginning to accommodate the names of the instruments – Flutes 1 & 2, Flute 3,
Oboes 1 & 2, English Horn – all the way down to Basses, then
the thick double line to show that this is the beginning, the
left-hand frame of the picture. Now the clefs and the time signature. There is no need for a key signature: contemporary
music, however conservative, modulates too much to make a key
signature meaningful. But the opening theme, Example 1 slightly
elaborated, on flute and oboe with a quiet dissonant background
of tremulous divided violins, is certainly in a kind of C minor.
I have written 'Molto moderato' at the top and the bottom of the
page, and also in the space below the horns and the space above
the first violins. Spaces (meaning in practice staves left empty)
between the instrumental groups makes for ease of reading. After
the statement of Example 1, the English horn gives out Example
4 with some notes very long and others very short, and a few
twirls and twiddles which sound facetious or sinister or both. It
is accompanied by the clarinets and bassoons, and their harmonies are a chromatic sliding from Example 3 (b) to (c) and back
again:

Mozart, Beethoven and even Elgar were luckier than we. They
had a commonly accepted harmonic language – the one taught
in Stainer's textbook – and a theme knew precisely what harmonization it required. This is no longer so. The accompaniment
of a theme is as much a special act of creation as the theme itself.

The cellos, with sharp punctuation from three muted trombones doubled by three basses plucked, take up Example 4 and
mix it with Example 5 and the last bar of Example 1. When
massed cellos sound, they seem always to wish to discourse an
extended melody, as though accompanying Pavlova, and I can

quell the tuneful urge only by making them drop to their bottom
string and accept the chore of giving a bass to the next statement
of Example 1:

That descent in tritonal fourths is, I foresee, in danger of being
employed as a mannerism. Yet I forehear the various possible
transformations of the last bar of Example 1 as the most characteristic sound of the movement.

Example 1 on clarinets in octaves is followed by violins, high,
divided, strident, crying Example 4 with a note of hysteria,
lifting it, rung by chromatic rung, to a high-held dissonance
(mostly, as you guessed, those tritonal fourths), while the whole
brass section punctuates with compressed versions of Example
3 (b):

In other words, superposed fourths in two different keys, bitonality encouraged by that last bar of Example 1. We now hear the
whole of Example 1 again, played in quavers by four horns in
unison, totally without nuances, while the kettledrums make an
ostinato out of the C D G of the first bar of Example 1. However
good or bad this music is, it at least accepts the principle of
unity: thirty-seven bars (near enough to the projected forty) built
out of the same minimal material. This is what is meant by
symphonic writing.

The movement proper can now begin – allegro vivo, in a
galloping time with sometimes two, sometimes three beats to the

bar. The flutes, and then the violins, carry Example 1 and its subsidiaries in a transformed rhythm:

By shortening the third note in the first bar, the opening of the theme is made to pulse out a three-beat rhythm, and this encourages the formation of a couple of new subsidiaries as accompanying figures:

EXAMPLE 7

The artistic problem is revealed not as how to expand but how to contract. With the colouristic resources of the orchestra, the drive of the trochaic rhythm, and the developmental potentialities of the themes themselves, I have the impression of an urgent narrative. The 'diabolic' flavour of the tritonal fourths is not much in evidence: the rhythms have tamed them:

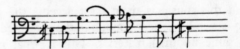

By now, as I more expected than hoped, the second subject group has emerged from my unconscious. There are two themes:

EXAMPLE 8

EXAMPLE 9

As is often the way with second subjects, these have a more melodic bias than Example 1 and its subsidiaries. Example 8 can be continued at some length. It is, in contrast with the first thematic group, in a major key, but it loses the C sharp and G sharp which define its A major tonality and seems to be too strongly influenced by the minor atmosphere which has persisted from the first bar on. But the accompaniment, based on the crotchet theme in the tenor of Example 7, is undubitably major, and the C and G natural of Example 8 sound like 'blue' inflections. If we were not committed to equal temperament, I should like the C and G to be a little sharper than they are. The flavour, certainly, is not at all minor. While Example 8 augments the three quavers of the first group into three crotchets, Example 9 augments the beat of the rhythm. Example 9 has a folky quality and even ends, like any regular popular song, on the tonic. But the tritones are ready to debauch it: it will not keep its innocence for long.

The existence of a shaped melody encourages, during the development section that follows, the formation of a bigger

melody. I have unconsciously been following Sibelius's example,
organizing thematic wisps into a new totality. While the rest of
the orchestra deforms Example 9 and tries to persuade it that it
belongs to the first thematic group, and the repeated dotted
crotchets of Example 8 hammer out the tritonal fourths, four
horns in unison, followed by clarinets, give this tune out very
suavely:

EXAMPLE 10

Clearly this is a synthesis of various fragments. Bars 1 and 2
come from the accompanimental crotchets of Example 7. The
supertonic–tonic drop in bar 3 is characteristic of Example 1.
Bars 7 and 8 are the bass of Example 9. The characteristic
supertonic–tonic is insisted on in what follows, bar 12 is a version
of bar 1 of Example 1, then the melody rises to the Neapolitan
sixth of Example 1 and ends with a descendent of fourths which
inverts bar 3 of Example 1. There is nothing new here; the
novelty lies in the mere fact of a lengthy melodic statement
proceeding under a strenuous development of six-eight material.
To confirm its melodic status, Example 10 has a codetta or
pendant which emphasizes that the melody has a right to a full
close on the tonic:

EXAMPLE 11

Clearly this is nothing more than a mixture of Example 4 and
the alternative cadence (Example 2) of the first two bars of

Example 1. It is heard on woodwind and is very coldly harmonized in superposed fourths.

The recapitulation has a double purpose: to exhibit once again the thematic fragments of the exposition (which means a naked dismantling of Example 10) and to draw the first and second thematic groups into the same rhythmic and tonal orbit. That the first and second groups should appear in the same key is not, in this post-Beethovenian epoch, very important, but it is essential that the two groups be unified in mode, either minor or major: preferably major, since the slow coda is to be in C minor. Examples 8 and 9 have in common a brief phrase – tonic, submediant, dominant (C A G) which is also to be found in Example 4: the major key and the Dorian mode share an unflattened sixth. If we emphasize the major mode by sounding the major third and tonic of a cuckoo call (taken from bar 1 of Example 9) we are, as will be seen when we reach the last movement, merely anticipating a feature to come and not suggesting a 'rural' programme – despite the restored folkiness of Example 9. The C A G which the major and Dorian versions of the scale of C share may be used, rallentando, to lead to the coda, which is mostly restatements of Example 10, first on solo viola, then on strings, with Example 1 as bass:

There are violent restatements of Example 11 on the full orchestra, with drums and cymbals:

The dissonances are not of arbitrary manufacture: they all derive from the superposed fourths of Example 1; but they reach an excruciating pitch which the composer finds it difficult to justify in terms of the emotional content of the movement. After a discord which contains all the notes of the chromatic scale, the English horn, unaccompanied, gives out the opening of Example 10, and repeats it in its lowest compass, while the violins, in their highest compass, restate Example 1 very coldly. The naked brass blare the rising fourths, ending on D flat, which fades to *niente*, and then the tritonal fourths – D flat A flat G D – drop to a final C.

I draw the double bar, the right-hand frame of the picture. I have spent about a month creating this movement, in the intervals of fiction-writing, reviewing, cooking, and being a husband and father. The concentration has been considerable, but odd passages have glued to them quite inconsequential memories – of a particular voice or face on television, a stab of heartburn, a cat licking my toes. The instrumentation went smoothly enough, except for the harp part, which is often more trouble than it is worth. All those enharmonic notations and comfortable disposition of chords, and often very little can be heard. It is time to compose the second movement.

Since the first movement has ended in a slow tempo – the coda, indeed, being a virtual slow movement in itself – it seems reasonable to place the scherzo next. I have, filed and waiting, all the themes I need. The main one is:

EXAMPLE 12

This at once suggests a variation which changes the time:

Thus, there will be a juxtaposition of double and triple time which matches one of the features of the first movement. Otherwise the two movements have nothing in common. In a scherzo one is entitled to play, show off, or permit the orchestra to show off, but the rule of unity is so deeply embedded in the symphonic structure that the play must play only on the surface, like foam. Evidently the motif to be developed here is contained in the opening bar of Example 12. But the rising fourth and third of bar 3 must be important, otherwise they would not have reappeared at the end of the three-four variant. What in fact emerge as the salient features of the movement are a rhythm –

(the *diabolus* has appeared again, but he is too comic to be dangerous) – and a pair of intervals:

The trio is not long in coming. There is a confused gamelan sound from strings, harp, piano, celesta and glockenspiel, and the wind plays three mock-pastoral themes simultaneously:

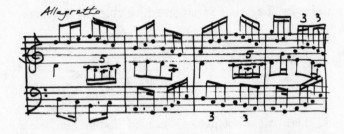

At the end of the trio these three themes, with the addition of another, are given to a string quartet which is interrupted occasionally by dissonances on the full orchestra. This is known as the true Beethovenian spirit. In the recapitulation of the scherzo the bass tuba is given a solo, the different sections of the orchestra compete with each in skirling on secondary sevenths in third inversion, everybody marches, the xylophone has a virtuoso passage, and the whole thing comes to a consonant end on the chord of G major.

Slow movements are difficult to write these days. We have no faith and are ashamed of naked sentiment; all that is left is an exhibition of psychosis. My intention, in an adagio of some 120 bars (crotchet = 60), was to express regret at the death of Dmitri Shostakovich, but there are no personal elegies in music, nor indeed are there in poetry: the nature of art is to generalize: Lycidas is a sea spirit, not Milton's friend King. The form should, like the second movement of Elgar's Second Symphony, be a marcia funebre, and there should be an attempt to evoke the feeling of Shostakovich's First Symphony in a brief scherzo-like interlude. But there is little marchlike about the movement, and there is nothing of Shostakovich there either. The opening theme is for strings and horns:

EXAMPLE 13

This sounds tonal, or modal, enough, but there is no real key centre. The lack of the sense of a tonic, meaning a sense of direction, disqualifies the theme as the opening of a funeral march, since a funeral march knows all too well where it is going. This theme reaches A flat major so that a minuscule dotted figure may appear:

EXAMPLE 14

The reiteration of Example 13 on full and angry orchestra leads to a kind of half-close on the chord of G sharp minor, first inversion, and then the rhythm of Example 13 and the dotted figure from Example 14 combine in the following:

EXAMPLE 15

And, after Example 13 has been developed a little, Example 15 is transformed into what amounts to a new theme:

EXAMPLE 16

Music occasionally possesses associations which are more than personal. A falling fifth, as in Example 15 and this new theme, suggests a bugle call, especially if it is played on a solo trumpet. A soft slow bugle call can only signal Retreat or Last Post. It seemed to me I had heard that first bar of Example 16 before – not, of course, on a parade ground or at a military cemetery, since no bugle could manage a major second. I eventually realized that, thirty years before in Gibraltar, I had set the words of Wilfred Owen – 'And bugles calling for them from sad shires' – to almost that identical theme:

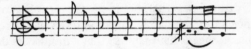

In other words, if there is a non-musical referent here, it has more to do with the slaughter of two world wars than with the death of a solitary composer. Hearing Example 16 in my head, I heard it as a melancholy statement on a solo trumpet, but on paper, externalized, it is for strings. The two bars go up a fifth, then up a fourth, in the manner of a fugal exposition, but bar 1 of Example 16 soon gets on to solo oboe – not quite a trumpet: the trumpet will come later. Meanwhile, on solo piano, there is a scherzando theme:

This is permitted to proceed for only two bars before the first bar of Example 16 comes back again on bassoon. Flutes and clarinets take up the scherzando passage, once more to be interrupted by Example 16 on horn (we are getting closer to the trumpet now), and it is muted trumpets, still trying to postpone the elegiac, which attempt a variation of the skittish demisemiquavers, helped by the xylophone. It is evidently a very facetious and perhaps vulgar passage, an attempt to avoid a serious meditation on death in battle. But now, with an accompaniment of divided upper strings, the English horn gives out a theme with bugle-call intervals in it:

EXAMPLE 17

Note the tendency to avoid the major third and hence confirm that the theme is in, as it seems to be, E flat major. We do not want, these days, the unambiguous blatancy of such modal assertion: the major third seems vulgar. The string accompaniment also avoids the third.

The second half of Example 17 is now taken up by the full orchestra, with clarinets and bassoons trying to counter the elegiac atmosphere by sounding the scherzando theme. There are some very angry dissonances, and then we are ready for Example 16 on a quiet solo trumpet before recapitulation of the main material, with Example 13 on woodwind, Example 16, fugato, on strings, and then a violent interruption from brass and percussion, which give out a distorted and mocking version of Example 17. All that remains to do is to give to woodwind and strings in alternation the kind of mirror chords Holst used in his 'Venus':

It is only now that I recall Holst's subtitle for that movement from *The Planets*: 'The bringer of peace'. There is more of a programme to my own movement than was clear to me at the time of writing it. Take the above sequence another step and we are back, though with different, more pacific, harmonies to Example 13, the opening of the movement. The muted trumpet will not permit peace to have the final word. It states and repeats the opening bar of Example 17, and the last chord shows that the movement, despite contrary evidence in its themes, has had no clear notion of its tonality.

The finale begins allegro giocoso with C D G on kettledrums, the identical notes of their first intervention in the first movement and, indeed, the first three notes of Example 1. The orchestra answers this drum solo with the quintuplet of Example 17. After a few bars of this antiphony two clarinets, with an accompaniment of side drum, mock the first bar of Example 17 in a bitonal canon:

EXAMPLE 18

But this is not the main theme of the movement. It is an attempt to discredit the elegiac before the main theme appears. It is also a device for presenting an accompanimental figure (top line, bar 6) which will be important later.

The main theme is first heard on two flutes, with strings strumming a chord of superposed fourths:

EXAMPLE 19

It is not much of a theme, but I claim no compositorial responsibility for it. The theme was, as far as I can judge, composed by William Shakespeare. In *Love's Labour's Lost*, the pedant Holofernes – a part I am convinced was taken by the playwright himself: Holofernes (also a cant term for the penis) is biblically related to Judith, the name of Shakespeare's younger daughter – has a long pedantic speech in prose, in which he extols the beauties of the poet Mantuan. 'Good old Mantuan,' he says. 'Who understandeth thee not loves thee not.' And then he compares the poet to the city of Venice, reciting, or singing, the following choice Italian:

> *Venezia, Venezia –*
> *Chi non ti vede, non ti prezia.*

You have to see Venice before you appreciate her; you have to read Mantuan before you can love him. And he ends his cadenza with six notes in a solmized notation: Ut re soh lah mi fa. These, in the key of C major, in staff notation, are those first six notes of the first flute in Example 19.

Shakespeare's theme is not so artless as it appears. It makes sense inverted (Example 20) and (Example 21) reversed. Repeated a tritone higher or lower (Example 22), it provides a kind of twelve-tone *Grundstimmung*:

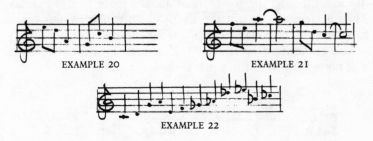

EXAMPLE 20   EXAMPLE 21

EXAMPLE 22

It certainly, in its various forms, provides enough material for the first theme group. It expresses unity with the opening theme of the whole symphony by sharing its first three notes with it. When the time for the second subject arrives, this too is provided by Shakespeare–Holofernes, for those two lines of Italian suggest the following tune:

EXAMPLE 23

The mood of the music is undoubtedly extrovert, even popular, and a mandoline (played by a versatile second violinist who discovered one at home) lends the right southern touch. Wine, revelry, no more war. But the brief development section tries to drag Example 19 and its variants into an area of sinister sound, exploiting the diabolic (we are back to those tritones of Example 1). The violins accept the notion of bitonality, but it is the harmless one of Example 18, suggesting Darius Milhaud and Provençal mirth, and not the (tritonal) interval of the air-raid siren. In other words, the elegiac or warlike is mocked once

again in the recapitulation. Example 18 is developed to its limit
with whoops on the high horns, and then there is a sudden
pause.

A solo piano plays an arpeggio of the major thirteenth, in the
manner of the late Lord Britten, many of whose themes were
made out of that arpeggio. A baritone soloist delivers a piece of
Latin, a line of Mantuan, and then, in the words of Holofernes,
praises the poet. He leaves it to a tenor soloist with a high range
(up to C) to sing the Italian lines about Venice to Example 23.
Then he reminds us that the six notes on which Example 19 is
based are the final statement of the Holofernes speech.

The orchestra now rejoices in Example 19 and its variants.
The notes blur in a trumpet bell-chime:

The horns blur the inversion, the trombones the reversion, and
then the whole ensemble blurs, chimes and clashes. We are
admitted to a kind of princely court, where Example 23 is converted into the music of a processional. Example 13 is cleansed
of its elegiac associations, and Example 14, on the horns, is
triumphantly baroque. The tenor and baritone are permitted to
turn themselves into clarinets and vocalize the bitonal passage
Example 18. Example 13 very joyously drowns them, but they
try again. The drowning task is now left to a crescendo on a
kettledrum, but the baritone stops the deafening roll with a
gesture. The piano sounds another arpeggio on the thirteenth,
and the baritone, in the words of Holofernes, invites us to listen
to something homelier. 'Enough of this. Will you hear instead
the dialogue that we two learned men have contrived concerning
the owl and the cuckoo?' We are at the end of the last scene of
Love's Labour's Lost. The strings, playing with the wood of their
bows, paint a couple of bars of a winter landscape. The strings,
playing with the bow, carve a miniature of spring. Winter is

presided over by the owl (the oboe twits), and spring by the cuckoo. At last the major third of Example 9 in the first movement is justified in terms of Beethovenian or Delian mimicry. The clarinet becomes a cuckoo. But the cuckoo, in its earliest song of the year, gives out a minor third. The wind instruments are ready for both, and the minor third is heard to be not an interval of gloom but a step on the way to the glory of summer. The horns (which, in a sense, are related to the cuckoo call, since the cuckold wears horns and is mocked by the cuckoo) can hardly distinguish between major and minor third, and the 'blue' thirds of Example 8 in the first movement are given their natural explanation.

The tenor and baritone share between them the words of the two songs that end *Love's Labour's Lost*. They make their melodies out of Examples 19 and 23. A winter phrase alternates with a spring phrase, and eventually tenor and baritone sing of winter and spring, the owl and the cuckoo, simultaneously. Cold (superposed fourths) and heat (tritonal fourths) are complementary aspects of the cycle of life. The orchestra leaves enunciating abstract musical patterns and blatantly illustrates the words of the conjoined songs. There is a riot of birdsong while the tenor tells of spring. The cuckoo which mocks married men blares major and minor on brass. Icicles hang by the wall (xylophones), Dick the shepherd blows his nail (breathy flute), Tom bears logs into the hall (deep clumsy brass: he drops some of them), milk is frozen (glockenspiel), coughing drowns the parson's saw or sermon (rim shot on side drum), roasted crabs hiss in the bowl (sizzle cymbal). In springtime the birds tread (woodwind), merry larks are ploughmen's clocks (aspiring solo violin out of Vaughan Williams), maidens bleach their summer smocks (the only dominant-seventh–tonic progression in the whole work). And then, unaccompanied, the vocal cadenzas which celebrate synchronically the owl and the cuckoo. Riotous coda based on Example 19, damnably and insouciantly dissonant. Then the spoken words of the baritone: 'The words of Mercury are harsh after the songs of Apollo. You that way, we this way.' Fortissimo C major chord on the full orchestra, with added seconds and sixths. The symphony is over.

The written score – 200 pages, the precise length of my first and very juvenile symphony in E major – is a curious diary of irrelevancies. I recall the smell of the air freshener in a New York hotel when looking at this page, the flight announcements in O'Hare airport, Chicago, are glued to that. The conscious act of concentration frees other segments of the senses and the mind to record the current of exterior life. What neither the score nor the tape of the first performance is able to recall is an emotion, or an emotional complex, of which the symphony is, in part or *in toto*, the objective correlative. We must now ask some very difficult questions about the relationship between music and life.

4
Music and Meaning

When I plan a novel I propose a verbal structure of some length – 80,000 words or more – in which all the elements are relevant to each other and nothing can be either added or subtracted without harming the whole. A work of art is traditionally characterized in terms of unity of conception and execution. Is my symphony a unified structure? Reluctantly I have to say no.

Take the scherzo. A fundamental rule of contrast demands that between two slow sections there should be a burst of speed, but quick is as comparative a term as slow, and if I had substituted a Brahmsian allegretto grazioso for my allegro molto there would have been no sense of unfitness. The allegro molto itself could have taken another form: its themes as it stands bear no structural relationship to those of the other movements. The fact that I introduce a scherzo at all has more to do with acceptance of a Beethovenian convention than artistic inevitability. When I point to the identity of the first three notes of the first theme of the first movement and those of the main theme of the last, I would, if I were honest, speak more of coincidence than of cunning. When analysts find that the slow movement, scherzo and finale of Beethoven's Fifth Symphony are alike in that they all begin with an arpeggio of a common chord, they are saying no more than that most pieces of music begin with a common chord. I fear that it is in the nature of symphonic analysts to seek unity where there is none: there is a conviction that, the symphony being the highest form of 'pure music' (that is, music unaided by words or an imposed programme), it ought to proclaim artistic unity throughout. In the classical period of the symphony unity did not matter.

In the post-classical period it did not always matter. The movements of a symphony are usually separate pieces, unlinked with their neighbours, and can be performed as such. The finale of one symphony can be substituted for that of another. Slow movements are interchangeable. A naive audience would accept a Brahms symphony consisting of the allegro of the Third, the adagio of the Second, the allegretto of the First and, as finale, the scherzo of the Fourth – even without the adjustment of keys in the interests of tonal unity – as a designed totality. This process could naturally be even more plausibly fulfilled with the symphonies of Haydn.

Any twentieth-century composer of a symphony is functioning at the tail end of the romantic tradition which began with Beethoven, unless, like Stravinsky or Prokofiev, he is invoking a self-conscious classicism. The romantics and post-romantics seek a formal unity of a kind which the symphony, in its traditional shape, rejects. Rococo symphonists like Haydn and Mozart were not aware that such unity had to be sought: the unity subsisted already in terms of the *function* of the music. I begin to tread hazardous ground. I have to use the word *meaning*. A Haydn symphony had a meaning for the social group which listened to it. A Mahler symphony had a meaning for the man who composed it. Here is the difference between the classical and romantic attitudes to art. But I am not sure, nor is anyone, what is meant by meaning.

Behind all music of an instrumental nature lies the dance, and behind the symphony lies the dance suite. A dance suite has an inevitable unity in terms of the nature of dance: the human body performs stylized movements which do not directly relate to biological or utilitarian action. Within the unity of function – that of accompanying dance – subsists the diversity which confirms unity: a gigue may be different from a gavotte and both different from a sarabande, but all three conjoin in demanding from the human body sets of stylized movements. To listen to a suite of dances is to invoke mental images of such movements and, perhaps more important, an overall abstract image of the social stability of which the dance is a symbol. The mating of man and woman is emblematized in most of the dance forms of the West; the crowded ballroom is a symbol of human society energetic but not bellicose; men and women move together in circles which stand for the cycle of life; the music to which they dance moves in a linear pattern which, with its beginning, middle and end, suggests purpose and progress. The dance is a figure of the motion of the heavens and the stability of divine order which human society ought to reflect.

The place of the rococo symphony is the concert salon, not the ballroom. There are auditors, not dancers. The body is immobilized and only the mind has freedom of movement. The music of the dance is too simple and stylized now, though a gracious tribute to its importance will regularly appear in the rococo symphonist's minuet and trio. The three other movements will, in a sense, apotheosize the dance (which was what Wagner said Beethoven did in his Seventh Symphony). Once having established a tempo - allegro or andante – they will no more move away from it than will a ballroom gavotte or allemande. The social stability symbolized in the dance is raised to a higher power in the rococo symphony. There may be a solemn slow introduction to remind us of a seriousness of musical purpose not to be sought in a mere collocation of dance numbers; the allegro that follows is the accompaniment to imagined human actions which no ballroom could accommodate; the slow movement synthesizes a gravity of physical movement and a lyrical lilt; the finale outdoes the opening allegro in its symbolization of human energy.

Within these structures there are opposed themes which the imagination can explain in terms of the basic binary patterns of human life: the two sexes which oppose and yet complement each other; action and contemplation; death and renewal; the reconciliation following the quarrel. The binary structure of the brain, which orders the continuum of experience into the opposed signs out of which human culture is made, finds, in a Haydn or Mozart symphony, a basic correlative. The rococo symphony has no room for the voice of the dissident which questions accepted order, unless it is the ritual protest of the licensed humorist. Haydn can crash out his unexpected fortissimo in the 'Surprise' Symphony, but this is no revolutionary cannon.

When we speak of the 'meaning' of a Haydn symphony, we

say no more than that it is an auditory symbol of stability. The music means the society of which it is an artistic product. The basic language, as opposed to the structure, is simple: it is made out of the two modes of the diatonic scale which eighteenth-century Europe accepted as the systematization of intelligible melodic movement. A good deal of early seventeenth-century music was still trying to emancipate itself from the old modal system of the Greeks, the Church, the folk; with Purcell in England and the court composers of the Sun King in France, the principle of a major and a minor mode, with no Dorian or mixolydian atavism, was firmly established. It was to prevail for over two centuries. It was the auditory correlative of a hierarchical capitalist society. And yet it was as arbitrary in origin as any other linguistic system.

The harmonies of Haydn and Mozart conform to nature. The notes of the major triad were not arbitrarily chosen for a concord: they were already implicit in the harmonics of any given note. The major triad built on to the basic note of the scale – the tonic, to which a melody gravitates when it wishes to end – is the static symbol of both natural and social stability. Yet music is not made out of the crass reiteration of that concord: the power of the concord is best affirmed by resisting it, though any such resistance contains the seeds of its own collapse. Every discord has not only to be resolved but prepared: it can only appear in an ambience of good manners, which are another emblem of the stable society. If the tonic is the Sun King of the scale, the chosen key of a symphonic movement is the Sun King's court, and however widely that movement may range in other keys, we must always end with obeisance to the central authority. A symphony is in C or D or E flat, and this means an acknowledgement, even in an extended work, of one centre: the key centre is an emblem of the authority which presides over the state's stability. Music is tension and resolution, over and over again, but the movement is as natural as any action of the body, and its counterpart is intellectual and moral as well as physical. It is to be found, for instance, in a discourse which resolves the tensions of objections to a thesis and ends in a declaration of logical truth.

All the above sounds formulaic, and indeed it was only by adhering to accepted formulas that Haydn could compose as

many symphonies, sonatas, concertos and quartets as he did. But
there is an element in music which cannot be prescribed and is
not easy to explain, and that is the element of creative genius.
There were wholly efficient symphonists of the Mannheim school
who have been wholly forgotten, while Mozart and Haydn are
a flourishing part of the repertory. One aspect of their genius is
the power to inflect the established trope in such a way that the
complacent image of social stability is briefly impaired: a value
is questioned, but the question is almost immediately withdrawn.
There is a discreet or cunning or hardly to be noticed intrusion
of the strange or idiosyncratic. The audience is given more than
it needs, and this is explicable only in terms of the entrance of
a private personality into a public domain. The image of order
in the last movement of the 'Jupiter' Symphony uses more counterpoint than the average listener, tired after the chase or the
campaign, thinks he needs. The twelve-tone bridge passage in
the finale of the G minor Symphony is not quite in the language
of the day; there are everywhere in Mozart inflections of the
accepted. When we say that such inflections are evidence of the
thrust of the private into the public we are making no more than
a negative statement. Personal utterances in music can be defined
only in terms of what they are not – unless, that is, we are
prepared to be shamelessly metaphorical.

I will not, if I can avoid it, use the term genius again. But I
would note that it is more often used of romantic composers
than of classical ones. The genius is the wild-haired flower of
dissidence; he rejects established order and smashes all its images. He offers his own personality instead of emblems of collective stability. Mozart's genius is so discreet that sometimes it
is hardly to be noticed; that of Berlioz, Wagner and Liszt is
assertive. Beethoven, despite the ikons of a wounded Titan de-
fying the thunder, is not quite the romantic genius. He is bred
out of the classical age. His genius looks two ways. I will not, if
I can avoid it, use the term genius again.

Beethoven may be regarded as the founder of the symphony
as intermittent personal statement. In the recapitulation of the
first movement of the Fifth Symphony he stills the relentless
allegro pace and interposes a solo oboe theme, adagio. Then he
resumes the hurry. What does this mean? It means he is

temporarily breaking the consistent rhythm of a public utterance: that oboe solo is not in conformity with the rhythm, therefore it must have a private significance. What is this significance? We do not know.

That this first movement is public music in the sense that a Haydn first movement is public music may well be questioned. Beethoven, like Mozart only more so, gives more than is needed – violent alternations of pianissimo and fortissimo, emphases apparently unjustified by the mere notes. Moreover, when he comes to the scherzo and finale he finds it necessary to link these two, and, instead of a development section in the finale, he repeats the trio of the scherzo. This assertion of the unity of the two last movements is, again, more than the public needs. The accepted forms which symbolized exterior order are submitting to what can only be termed the onslaught of the personal, but what the personal message is – again, we cannot say.

There are four symphonies of Beethoven which will yield to the jumbling process already mentioned: you can, for an uninstructed audience, take the first movement of the First, the second of the Second, the third of the Fourth and the fourth of the Eighth and present them very plausibly as a fourfold entity. And you can do the same thing three more times with what is left. But in the remaining symphonies you cannot afford to interchange, despite the example of concert promoters of Beethoven's own day, who would, with the composer's connivance, present the slow movement of the Seventh in every possible context. Beethoven was concerned, as Haydn and Mozart did not have to be, with that unification of the symphony which became a preoccupation of the Romantics and which resulted in the ultimate collapse of the form. For the anomaly is that the rococo symphony exhibited merely the right selection of genres, like the dance suite before it, and achieved unity through conventional contrasts of mood. Once Beethoven, and the Romantics after him, sought an indissoluble totality of form, they could find it only through the intrusion of the personal or the imposition of a programme.

Let us consider the unity of the 'Eroica', the Pastoral and the Ninth. The mere student of the form of the 'Eroica' will find satisfaction in its unity of key – all four movements are in three flats – but few listeners have absolute pitch. The unity of the 'Eroica' is extra-musical: the work approaches programme music. The first movement is expansive, active, aspirant and full of violent contrasts of volume and accent; it ranges over a wide terrain of tonalities; we have already been told by the composer himself that a great man (not Napoleon, not after his execution of the duc d'Enghien) is being celebrated. The second movement is explicitly a marcia funebre – a public funeral, the interment of the same great man. The finale is a set of variations on a theme borrowed by Beethoven from his own *Prometheus* ballet music. We suspect the influence of Plutarch's *Lives*, which we know Beethoven read and reread. Plutarch has a binary biographical method: the life of a historical hero is followed by the life of a mythical one. It is fair to assume that Beethoven's scherzo has something to do with Prometheus. After all, the great historical figure was already dead at the beginning of the second movement, and there is now only myth to call upon. We may, if we wish, hear the flames of the fire stolen by Prometheus in the scherzo, and, in the trio, the horns of the gods giving chase.

The unity of the Pastoral Symphony is self-confessedly extra-musical: we are even told what to see and feel and hear – birdsong, a brook with a muddy bottom, a peasant square dance, thunder, rain, lightning, a rainbow, a shepherd's song after the storm. As for the Ninth, we can ignore analysts' assertions of the primacy of tonal unity, with D minor struggling towards D major. I once heard a private performance of the choral movement pushed down to C major, to ease the problems of the sopranos. Very few noticed. The secondary unity is certainly one of bulk: the first three movements are of a length proportionate to the massive finale, but the final unity is external and, indeed, almost literary. The opening of the last movement is a graphic presentation of a structure in search of a theme. The themes of the preceding movements are paraded in turn, only to be rejected by the wordless recitative of the basses. And then literature takes over entirely.

Post-Beethovenian symphonists have followed the master on the road to formal unification (not Brahms, of course) by recalling themes, as in the Fifth, or imposing, as in the Pastoral, an extra-musical programme. César Franck made of the sonata and symphony a kind of abstract cyclical drama, with thematic reminiscence suggesting the encoding of a private message. Tchaikovsky, very blatantly, bases his Fifth Symphony on a 'motto theme', heard in a gloomy or violent E minor and finally in a brassy, vulgarly triumphant E major. Dvorak, in his 'New World' Symphony, takes advantage of the fact that all his main themes can be harmonized with the same common chord and hence can intrude anywhere. The further we travel from the public assurances of the rococo age, the more we have to face questions of meaning, expressed in such questions as 'Why does this theme reappear at this point?' and 'Why do the dynamics here seem excessive?' and 'Why this sudden change of tempo?' We are struggling with a kind of semantics of music. We are treating the symphony as an enigmatic autobiography. We end with the symphonies of Mahler, wherein the appearance of a hurdy-gurdy tune in a tragic context has to be explicated by Freud (between trains), and the language of music makes claims to be as explicit a system of signs as the language of the novel.

This brings me back to my own symphony, to which, in the preceding chapter, I have already applied untenable metaphors. I was analysing it in the manner of the programme note or record sleeve. Because the medieval musicologists described the mode beginning on B and having F natural as its fifth as *modus diaboli*, I have pretended to find 'heat' in a discord built on tritones. Because the chord of superposed fourths denies the stable or homely affirmation of the triad, I have dubbed it 'cold'. Such terms have no meaning. If we approach the whole of the first movement in terms of a meaning, we shall be foiled, finding only themes of opposed character working in a structure built on the age-old principle of tension and release. Yet it will be said that the composition of an elaborate piece of music can only be justified if it is the expression of 'sincere emotion', whatever that is, and all else is mere note-spinning. But in note-spinning, presumably, there is no principle of selection; yet my themes are neither artificially contrived nor randomly chosen. I am prepared to find listeners making an emotional or even pictorial response to the music, but I do not think this is more than subjective fancy. I believe that the majority of composers are too preoccupied with the building of structures to concern themselves with 'emotion'.

I believe that, in the most general sense imaginable, music can have emotional referents, but these are not to be related to the *causes* of particular emotional experiences. The major mode can be happy, and its major third can be depressed to convey gloom. The tread of a funeral march or swirl of a waltz will convey, through associations, feelings of simple sorrow or simple elation. Upper partials on trumpets have a stimulating effect on the nerves. But I do not think we can go much further. To claim for music the capacity to present, with the explicit subtlety of literature, a complex narrative or a mystical revelation, seems to me to be a matter of imposed and often arbitrary non-musical associations. On the other hand, I do not deny that there are cerebral experiences of a nature too complex to be susceptible of expression through any medium except that of music. But no one knows as yet how this is done, and it is as well to be quiet about the matter. Since the beginning of the romantic revolution, music, having moved away from the dance (and therefore, according to Ezra Pound, risked atrophy), has either had to call on other arts, especially literature, to explicate its private messages, or else, as we shall see later, it has claimed the right to take over the function of literature.

As a literary practitioner, I am not prepared to allow this claim. But, referring for one last time to my own symphony, I am prepared to admit that only literature could solve my formal problems. I had to call on Shakespeare in my finale, not only for a musical theme but for words as well, and the nature of the words could convince me that I had achieved some kind of unity. The 'blue' thirds of the first movement were justified by an eventual cuckoo. An image of death in the third movement (if the falling fifth is really a bugle blowing over military crosses) is driven out by an assertion of the cyclical renewals of nature. Music limps, but words give it a crutch. Apollo needs Mercury.

Finding in music – and now I mean music without words – properties which had previously been the monopoly of literature began with the worshippers of Beethoven, and we had better now consider what the Beethovenians thought they had found. His mature sonatas, quartets and symphonies are created out of the basic inheritance of music – tension and resolution. But from the viewpoint of the baroque or rococo, the old stability of Bach or Haydn, the tensions seem exaggerated – through the idiosyncratic use of dynamics, gradations of volume, unexpected changes in tempo – and we gain the impression of personal conflict. The conflict is prolonged, and when resolution comes it is delayed and hard-won. Periods of peace balance phases of struggle, and slow movements are represented as visions of beatitude. The struggle is not physical (it is not – though knowing Beethoven's personal grossness we cannot be absolutely sure – Martin Luther fighting costiveness); it can only be moral, an attempt to win through to the light of the good after wrestling with the forces of darkness. Beethoven's private despairs and triumphs confirm this, as does his choice of a theme of inspiring moral content in his solitary opera – the death of tyranny, the fidelity of a woman who is also a lioness. We are told that the overture known as 'Leonora' no. 3 contains the whole opera: so it may, if we know the opera already.

During the nineteenth century, the Beethovenians – like Sir George Grove in England – had no doubt of the moral content of the great instrumental works. Beethoven had found the universal symbols for man's struggle with evil and his attainment of the celestial vision. This view of the composer as the sublime custodian of ultimate values was sustained well into our own century. The trouble began with the Nazis, who, being Germans, had more right to Beethoven than anybody, and who found in his work precisely those values discovered by an earlier age of humanists. The commandant of an extermination camp could spend the day supervising the consignment of Jews to the ovens, and then go home to weep tears of pure joy at the divine revelations of sonata or symphony – his flaxen chubby daughter at the keyboard, the fine record-player which was the due of his rank. On a summer evening in London in 1942, on that identical evening in Berlin, there were performances, both deeply moving and loudly applauded, of the Choral Symphony. Hitler's favourite opera was *Die Meistersinger*, and this preference has not sullied our own love of that masterpiece. It was always nonsense to proclaim that Beethoven's music was about the brotherhood of man, Jew and Gentile, or mystical union with the god of the liberals. If fascists and democrats found, as they did, the same matter for exaltation, then music cannot be about morality.

It is too easy to solve the problem by asserting that music is as purely physical an experience as the taste of an apple. The Nazis and their enemies undoubtedly met in an identity of response to life-enhancing tastes and odours, but a Schubert song or a Brahms sonata is a mental artefact and not a perfume or a nutrient. We are forced back to the basic situation: the content of music is tension and release, and its non-musical referents lie in a sphere of generalities that may be rolled into the arena of a political or moral tenet, but in itself music is apolitical and amoral.

The reader should now be heartily tired of this glib talk of tension and resolution. It leads us only to the prenatal experience of the maternal heartbeat and, in infancy, the presence or withdrawal of the maternal voice. It is the mere principle of communication, which depends on an opposition of signs, and avoids what communication is about. If music communicates, and we are assured that it does, it is a genuine system of signs, a semiotic organization, and we must try to see how it functions.

5
Meaning Means Language

A quark is defined as 'any of three hypothetical subatomic particles having electric charges of magnitude one-third or two-thirds that of the electron, proposed as the fundamental units of matter.' The word is taken from James Joyce's *Finnegans Wake*, where the gulls are ironically hailing the impotent King Mark of the Tristan legend: 'Three quarks for Muster Mark!' It is very nearly an arbitrary borrowing (the *three* qualifies total randomness). In Joyce the vocable is imitative, in physics it is a deliberately chosen counter whose phonetic content has nothing to do with what it defines. It is a typical word, in other words. Saussure, the father of modern linguistics, emphasized the arbitrary nature of words. The iconic word, like *moon* or *little*, where the nature of the vowel suggests an imitation of what is described, is very rare in language. Words are overwhelmingly seen to be arbitrary bundles of phonemes, or speech sounds, to which meanings are attached – either by fiat (as with *quark*) or by historic or prehistoric tradition, as with the greater number of words in the human vocabulary. These are the units of the most efficient system of communication mankind possesses.

Does music have comparable units? Evidently not. It has notes, and it has chords, and it has, in comparison with the number of words in even the smallest lexicon, very few of these. A note is atomic, like a phoneme. That word *quark* has, as a spoken unit, four phonemes for the British and five for the Americans, who pronounce r in it. To get the equivalent of a word in music you must choose a phrase of two or more notes; alternatively (an advantage language does not have and which, as I shall show later, literature envies) you can sound several

notes simultaneously. Your basic musical unit can be extended
in time or be virtually timeless:

That, as most readers will recognize, is the so-called mystic chord
of Scriabin – an item in his musical vocabulary which had its
own significance for the composer and has had rather less for his
listeners.

Can a meaning – that is, a referent or item in the outside world
– be attached to a musical phrase as it can be attached to a
bundle of phonemes? The answer is yes, and the process can be
quite as arbitrary as with *quark*. Wagner invented the principle
of the leitmotif, and for his *Ring* he contrived a great number of
musical phrases which have referents glued to them. I could
follow his example and say: 'I am about to make a statement on
the keyboard. Here are the lexical items of the statement. The
common chord of C means I, me, myself. The mystic chord of
Scriabin means kill or kills. The diminished seventh, any diminished seventh, means my wife. What am I now saying?'

The statement will be understood, as will the other available
orderings of the chords – I kill myself; I kill my wife; Kill I my
wife? – but it is obvious that this is not the way music operates.
The duration of a chord – crotchet, minim or semibreve – is of
immense importance to a composer, but the duration of a word
is a matter of mere rhetoric to the speaker: it is prosodic, or
suprasegmental, and it cannot even be indicated in conventional
script. Again, the first chord could be played pianissimo, the
second mezzo piano, and the last fortissimo – mere devices of
eccentric rhetoric in speech, but possessing a precise purpose in
the statements of the musician.

In fact, the basic materials of the musical vocabulary are the purely suprasegmental ones of speech. Matters of speed, vocalic prolongation and, to a large extent, of intonation are not fundamental to the communication of verbal meaning, but it is out of these elements that music is made. A musician, too, would totally reject the notion that meanings can be attached arbitrarily to notes, as they are to words. He might accept that the personal pronoun, as representing the firm centre from which the world is surveyed, the one item in the universe whose existence we cannot doubt, finds a correlative in a major triad. The major triad, being made of the lower harmonics of any given note, is a fact of nature, a basic reality. The diminished seventh, as used to designate 'my wife', suggests dubiety, since it is a chord which could belong to any one of eight keys and, being homeless until resolved, it has connotations of anxiety. It cannot *denote* 'my wife', but it can suggest an attitude to her. The Scriabin chord is an undoubted discord, and it might well serve to symbolize violent dissolution, but it is probably, especially nowadays, not violent enough. What the composer would certainly strongly reject would be the arbitrary use of the major triad to mean 'kill', but he might not object to it as a correlative of death, so long as the death were both peaceful and desired by the dying.

It is perhaps because the composer knows, through instinct and experience, what phrases and what chords can be used in the setting of words in song and opera, that he ascribes to such musical components meanings that do not need to be particularized by words. Before music became capable of the kind of instrumental independence which could produce a symphony, it relied, for its longer structures, on the setting of words, secular or sacred, and it learned a sort of consonance of phrase, or chord, and verbal meaning. Take away the words, an easier process than setting them, and the verbal meaning remains, but it seems now to be purely a musical meaning. Out of this is bred the romantic arrogance of Berlioz and Strauss, which holds that musical language can replace verbal language and the art of music can take over the art of literature.

The arrogance of romanticism was encouraged by the growth of musical resources in the romantic period. The verbal resources of the great poets of the past, from Homer to Shakespeare, do not seem to us to be inferior to our own, but, in Homer's time, music hardly existed except as modal monody, and, in Shakespeare's, it is hard to think of a Byrd or a Weelkes being able to match the intensity and complexity, as well as violence, of *Hamlet* or *King Lear*. It is, as we all know, highly dangerous to speak of the *progress* of music in the historical period, since art does not progress, the limitations of his material are never a source of frustration to the artist, and every age believes it has achieved the highest conceivable pinnacle of art. But the fact is that music has always depended, while literature has not, on technical innovation, and the nineteenth-century composers were the beneficiaries of immense advances in both the linguistic and instrumental resources of their art.

When we play the *Well-Tempered Clavier* of Bach, we are made to realize how comparatively novel are the blessings of the tempered scale. As a boy, I thought 'well-tempered' was a whimsical epithet for a keyboard that did not fight back at the performer, and it was only slowly that I realized that the scale in nature was not the same as the scale on the piano in the living room. By a cunning flattening of fifths, our instruments have been made to accommodate an entire cycle of keys impossible to the virginals that Shakespeare's mistress played. The sonatas of Beethoven are adventures that range through all the keys and exploit devices of modulation that could have had no meaning for John Bull or Orlando Gibbons. In nature G flat and F sharp are different notes: in the tempered scale they are the same, and they permit movement from one key to another by means of auditory puns. The dominant seventh of D flat changes its G flat to F sharp (a pure matter of notation) and becomes the augmented sixth, whereby we land at once into the distant key of C major. The diminished seventh provides access to any one of four major or four minor keys: Samuel Butler called it the Clapham Junction of the keyboard.

The pianoforte for which Beethoven composed was one of the great technical innovations of the Napoleonic age, and it was Beethoven who, using a valved horn in his Ninth Symphony, prefigured the revolution in the orchestra. The classical horns and trumpets were confined to the bugle calls of the harmonic series, but, with the provision of valves, they had the chromatic scale at their disposal. What the possibilities of the romantic orchestra are we begin to see, spectacularly, in the *Symphonie Fantastique* of Hector Berlioz, composed only a few years after the death of Beethoven, but those possibilities are forced into fulfilment by the pressure of imposed literary programmes, not by the inner urgings of musical inspiration alone. The *Symphonie Fantastique* uses all the devices of Beethovenian language, leaps about the entire terrain of the keys, exploits the mimetic possibilities of the instruments – *ranz des vaches* on English horn, multiple kettledrums for thunder, eight harps for a ballroom scene, drumrolls before the blade of the guillotine falls, squeak of an E flat clarinet at the witches' sabbath, tolling bells while trombones and tubas intone the *Dies Irae* – and all in the service of the story of a young artist who has lost his mistress and sees her apparition through opium clouds. The occasional clumsiness of the music, which all the commentators admit, is excused by the daring of the conception. It is as if a novelist, in despair at the inadequacy of words to convey his vision, has taken a crash course in music because music is the only other available outlet. This is precisely what Berlioz intends to demonstrate: the superiority of music to literature as a literary medium.

The conviction that the romantic orchestra and the resources of the post-Beethovenian vocabulary were eloquent enough to absorb the materials of literature was corroborated by the new French view of Shakespeare. Berlioz, like Dumas, was overwhelmed in the 1830s by the performances of Shakespeare given by a visiting English company in Paris. (In the company was a young Irish actress, a Miss Smithson, with whom Berlioz fell symphonically nay fantastically in love.) It seemed to many that the greatness of Shakespeare was impaired by the theatrical conventions forced upon him by his own era. The situations were magnificent, the psychology profound, the speeches sublime, but what Shakespeare had really wished to write was not plays but novels. The romantic novel not existing in his time, only the picaresque, he was compelled to waste the wealth of his imagination on a far inferior form. It was a pity, but it was possible for Berlioz to put everything right by translating Shakespeare into music. And so he composed *Roméo et Juliette*, using words where it seemed necessary to call on a chorus, but handing over

Mercutio's Queen Mab speech to the orchestra, and turning Romeo and Juliet into respectively a clarinet and an oboe.

Berlioz similarly remade part of Byron's *Childe Harold* – an act of arrogance wholly justified, since the concerto–symphony *Harold in Italy* (the old genres are certainly dying) is superior as art to the poem. He also remade Virgil in *Les Troyens*, one of the great operatic achievements of the century. There seems to be a romantic perverseness here, with an English dramatist turned into a symphonic novelist and a Roman epic poet converted into a dramatist. But the division between post-Gluckian opera and symphonic fiction is not so great as it appears. The words on the stage are a mere pretext for the psychological complexities proceeding in the orchestra. We cannot doubt that the orchestra is discoursing particularities about human relationships, because the words up there on the stage are telling us so, if we can hear the words. The orchestra may, as in Wagner and Strauss, drown the words, but we can look up the words in the printed libretto. The words are a pretext for the sounds, which are the true statement, and as the statement is analytical there is little room on the stage for the dramatic action which denies the need for analysis. Eventually it will be unnecessary for Tristan and Isolde to do more than repeat each other's name, while the avowals of love, and indeed love's physical fulfilment, are left, with a certainty of eloquence that no mere words could encompass, to the players in the pit. It does not matter whether you hire a theatre or a concert hall. The declamations of the singers and the printed declaration of the content of the *Symphonie Fantastique* share the same pretextual function. One word will be enough to call the music down from the sky of generality to the wrist of the particular.

The arrogance of Berlioz led to the greater arrogance of Strauss – meaning Germanic as opposed to merely Gallic. There comes a point in his opera *Salome* where it is clear that sung words have no further function. Salome gets the shorn head of John the Baptist and kisses the lips which are no longer living flesh but mere morphology. Her words are redundant: the huge orchestra is perfectly capable of dealing with all that pseudo-biblical imagery. Ring down the curtain. The orchestra will tell us when the soldiers are crushing Salome to death under their shields.

The orchestra can tell us everything. We have entered the world of the symphonic poem.

The symphonic poem represents the inevitable terminus of the development of the Beethoven symphony. Artistic unity, no longer to be fulfilled in the rococo manner through a mere selection of genres, has to be found in a literary programme, and the symphonic poem may be said to begin with the 'Eroica'. Franz Liszt saw very clearly the direction the symphony had to take – a three-movement work like the *Faust Symphony* and a tone poem like *Les Préludes* differ only in the commitment of the one to the depiction of character and the other to the expression of (rather banal) poeticisms – but Richard Strauss consumed the possibilities of the new form in the huge *Ein Heldenleben*.

This is, however much we may cry out against the excessive orchestral forces, the vulgarity, and the rampant egoism, a very great work. We have all reached the point of being able to take in the music as character and narrative without having to consult the programme notes. It is genuine epic and genuine autobiography. It is the complete vindication of the new form, but very little can be done after it. *Don Quixote* is successful in a different way. The concept is brilliant – fantastic variations on a theme of knightly character, as Strauss himself puts it in the subsidiary title – but the significance of the enterprise for the composer seems to be the extent to which the world of solid objects can be absorbed into music. It is not just a matter of making eight muted horns mimic the bleating of sheep but rather an implied declaration that music can give us the Platonic ideal of the bleating of sheep. The representative arts are usually humble in relation to their referents. Art, after all, is inferior to nature. But music is the mind of God, or Strauss, and the outside world is transfigured once it is transformed into organized sound. Strauss was arrogant enough (or perhaps it was ironic arrogance) to assert that anything could be represented in music, and hence transfigured to a higher order of reality. It should be possible to represent a glass of lager, and to make it clear who the brewer is; to set knives and forks on the table of the musical imagination and show them to be either silver or pewter.

This sort of thing can, in fact, be done and ought to be done. Strauss demonstrated his method in the dinner music for *Le*

Bourgeois Gentilhomme (used as the prelude to and justification of *Ariadne auf Naxos* – the most brilliant of Hofmannsthal's confections). When Rhine salmon is served, we hear Wagner's Rhine leitmotif; the roast lamb comes from that flock in *Don Quixote*. It has to be extra-musical or quasi-literary unless a label is directly attached to the representation. In William Walton's *Belshazzar's Feast* we are told which gods the Babylonians are praising, and the gods are carried in procession – strokes on the anvil for the God of Iron, slapstick for the God of Stone, xylophone for the God of Wood (more etymology than sound), brass for the God of Brass, woodwind for the God of Silver. A slapstick is not made of stone, nor are flutes and oboes silver, though a metaphor will make their tones silvery. Musical images thus demand a diversity of method – the literal, the associative, the metaphorical – but there is no referent which defeats them, so long as words are somewhere around.

We ought to note that practically all the developments in romantic and post-romantic music spring out of attempts to represent, or interpret, phenomena traditionally left to the other arts. A great deal has been written, including whole books, on the chord which opens the Prelude to *Tristan*:

Here we have a prophecy of the collapse of traditional tonality. Though that chord could be glossed as an ordinary secondary seventh in the key of F sharp or G flat major (notated differently, of course), it is revealed as not belonging to any recognizable key. The love of Tristan and Isolde is compounded of elements which deny traditional fealty and even the life-enhancing ends of the sexual relationship. In *Finnegans Wake* the seagulls may mock King Mark with their quark, but here the situation is tragic because disruptive of social order. Wagner is impelled to the formulation of a harmonic system which denies a fixed centre, and he opens the door for Schönberg and atonalism.

Romanticism, after fulfilling itself grandiosely in Strauss, had either to be denied by Paris or broken down and remade into a new system by Vienna. Debussy could not compose music without employing extra-musical referents, whether derived from literature, the pictorial arts, or nature herself. In his two volumes of *Préludes* he is prepared to represent Mr Pickwick or General Levine or seaside minstrels or a girl with flaxen hair, but his mode of representing them denies their humanity and converts them into impersonal objects, like heather or fog or the west wind or the perfumes of night invoked by Baudelaire. The musical language has to deny the hierarchy of the diatonic scale and its harmonies, since we are not in a world where social values apply. A chord is a block of sound followed by identical blocks of sound further up or lower down the scale: there is none of the old syntax which deferred to a tonal centre. New scales have to be manufactured or imported – like the whole-tone scale of Java – and the old modes are revived. But the new language is not there to serve a self-referring art. Debussy is just another postrococo composer, like Berlioz, claiming to absorb the external world into music.

The atonal revolution of Schönberg derives ultimately from *Tristan*, but it was when studying the score of *Salome* in 1907 – an opera which presents the final breakdown of order – that he observed for the first time harmonies whose roots could not be defined and a mere pretence of coherent language. It could be said that Schönberg's democratization of the chromatic scale, with every one of the twelve semitones equal to each other, was a denial not merely of the hierarchy by which the Austro-Hungarian Empire of Haydn and Mozart had subsisted, but a rejection of nature herself, since nature does not recognize a scale artificially tempered to equal intervals. It is certain, I think, that atonal music, even when structured according to the rules of serialism, has referents of breakdown – not only in society but in the individual psyche itself.

The test for evaluating music, ever since the death of Beethoven and perhaps even before his death, has been the degree of fidelity with which it has interpreted an extra-musical subject matter. There was a period of roughly a century and a half when instrumental music could subsist in a kind of self-referential purity – the period of the baroque and the rococo. Certain assumptions about God and human society permitted the production of a kind of music – whether a fugue, a passacaglia or a symphony – which was an image of accepted order. With the coming of Beethoven there was an attempt to continue this tradition, but it depended on a view of social stability which could not last. The new philosophy found its centre in the individual, and the new music was a mirror of this. The workings of the individual psyche are best presented in literature, and it was to literature that the new musicians went for their themes and structures.

I use the term literature loosely. I mean by it the representation of human thought, feeling and action – biographical or fictional – preferably in words but acceptably in media where the verbal element is minimal or even non-existent. In the sense that ballet, which is wordless, and film, which can be wordless, are art forms derived from the drama – traditionally a branch of literature – and depend on character and action, they are literary enough and, when music is applied to them, demand what may be called literary music. Thus, music treats film as it treated drama: it tries to convert it into a kind of novel. Film is a popular art form which uses music to underline setting and action and to suggest unspoken currents of thought and feeling, but, unlike Wagnerian music drama, it cannot permit the narrative to be absorbed into the music. It is far closer to the literal melodrama (not necessarily the debased form which made the term pejorative) of the Victorian age.

In listening to the music of the cinema, we gain a diluted and popular idea of the vocabulary now available to the not absolutely serious composer. I have written a little film music myself, and know that the exigencies of the medium will not permit music to be too original or even too interesting. It must not intrude. It is permitted very few complete statements. Like a diffident speaker in the presence of an arrogant one, it must be prepared to be cut off in the middle of a sentence. It can rarely use an accepted form, like fugue or passacaglia. But it has an eclectic language, and this never, except in historical films where the music becomes part of the action, evokes the age of stability. Background music in the manner of Haydn or Mozart must always draw attention to itself as primary and not ancillary art. The sounds required are those of 'literary' music.

We can particularize and say that the harmonic language of film music is mostly that of early Debussy – *The Blessed Damozel* rather than *Jeux*. There are plenty of secondary sevenths, and a sequence of these will be suitable for any meditative passage. Atonalism is to be admitted only when there are visual images of alienation. In composing the music for an Italian documentary called *The Eyes of New York*, I was drawn to the abandonment of a key centre when the film showed the poor and outcast, the young drugged, or the sculpture of George Segal. But visions of skyscrapers call for major tonalities with added notes (seconds, sixths, sevenths, ninths) and the kind of melodic nobility which owes more to Rachmaninov than to Beethoven. There is, despite its contrived functionalism, a certain honesty in this kind of music. It represents what the ordinary listener can accept as intelligible language, and no composer can cut in and justify extravagances on the grounds of some new theory. An affirmation (Manhattan; the Rockies; a man satisfying thirst) cannot be accompanied by that Scriabin chord: a major triad is called for.

When composing film music, the musicians of our age are compelled to use an eclectic language which they must regard as old-fashioned. Writing 'seriously' they have to abandon eclecticism; they are forced into making a choice which excludes old-fashioned tonality and uses a loose atonality or a serialism derived from Schönberg or Messiaen. There is also a view of music which sees composition as an exploration of the nature of sound or, with John Cage, denies a distinction between the structured sounds of music and the noises of the external world. There is no generally accepted aesthetic of music, and this can do the art no good.

I have tried, for my own enlightenment, to use most of the musical idioms available today, from the Broadway show song to the rarefactions of Boulez, and I am disturbed by the lack of a synthesis. Music is no longer sure of itself. In the nineteenth century an attempt was made by Johannes Brahms to restore the old symphonic vision of stability, just as, in Edwardian England, Edward Elgar fixed an image of imperial serenity (though more scarred and hysterical than many suspect) before the darkness set in. But the real currents of musical development lay elsewhere. Music might have pretended, with Berlioz and Strauss, to absorb literature, but in fact it had turned itself into an adjunct to literature – critical, illustrative. Mozart was the last of the great composers.

It was, I suppose, a doubt about the capacity of music to provide me with a language that drove me to the craft of the novel, where there are solidities of character and *récit* and corresponding semantic and syntactical solidities. But, if literature has done so much for music, it may well be that music can do things for literature which only the musically trained *littérateur* is capable of envisaging. We can at least speculate about this.

6

Under the Bam

Whether William Shakespeare could sing high tenor or play on the viol-de-gamboys we shall never know. Whether he could write and read music we shall never know either, despite the main theme of the last movement of my symphony, or Edgar's solmized ending of a scene in *King Lear*, where he contemptuously gives out the first four notes of the 'big tune' in Richard Addinsell's *Warsaw Concerto*. This may be the throwing of dice and not caring what number, or note, comes up. That Shakespeare worked among musicians and knew what musical instruments looked like, and even how they functioned, we do not doubt. He presents, in one of his sonnets, a very closely observed picture of a lady playing the virginal, though he errs in his use of the term 'jacks'. When Lady Macbeth talks of screwing courage to the sticking place, the image is drawn directly from one of Shakespeare's actor colleagues tuning his lute. Shakespeare wrote words for singers, though, despite the claims of bardolaters, he was not the greatest lyrist of all time. Ben Jonson was better, and the common people know it, or used to. Everybody could once sing 'Drink to me only', but no pub closing-time ever resounded to 'Take O take those lips away'.

Shakespeare was a typical literary man in his appreciation of music, his willingness to rhapsodize or even philosophize over it: his type is as old as the two arts. But with Dr Samuel Johnson begins a phase in which it is permissible for a man of letters to despise music as empty noise. When Boswell spoke of the affective power of music, how it could make him weep or wish to rush into battle, Johnson said: 'I would never listen to it if it made me such a fool.' And yet Johnson had one of the finest ears of his age – sharp to hear what he was not intended to hear, and greatly concerned with euphony in both prose and verse. He composed both in his head, making the ear and not the eye the arbiter of sonic excellence. He seems, like many of his unmusical literary successors, to have regarded melody as poetic statement divested of its sense. Even writers who have tolerated music, or professed to be ravished by it (the regular stance of the Romantics), have heard it as affective sound which, since it lacked verbal meaning though it possessed stress and intonation, could be animal or angel or both but was not strictly human.

The Johnsonian attitude to music has persisted in the records of literature, and perhaps the limit of unmusicality was reached by the most musical of poets, Algernon Charles Swinburne. Swinburne was once treated to a performance of 'Three Blind Mice' on the piano and told that it was a song of sixteenth-century Rome. He professed to hear in it 'the cruel beauty of the Borgias'. Being ignorant about the frontier between music and poetry, he was capable of composing verse in which verbal euphony was a substitute for sense. 'Time with a gift of tears, grief with a glass that ran.' Sense, as T. S. Eliot remarked, requires an exchange of attributes, but no one ever concerned himself overmuch with sense in Swinburne. You can substitute, for what Swinburne really wrote, lines like these in the spring chorus from *Atalanta in Calydon*, and few will notice the nonsense:

> And the broad-browed farthingale timorous
> Is new-encaged in Didymus,
> For the rage is seethed in the florined aces,
> The songless Virgil who scratched the pane.

Of the ill-treatment of music by other poets, some of whom perhaps found justification for musical philistinism in the example of Swinburne, it is enough to mention A. E. Housman and W. B. Yeats. Housman raged at Vaughan Williams's song cycle *On Wenlock Edge*, which provides Housman's verses with the passion they lack unset, and would have forbidden composers to touch *A Shropshire Lad* at all if he could. Yeats is the supreme example of a major poet with a defective ear, but his intermittent hostility to music may have been the consequence of a trauma incurred when he heard three thousand boy scouts play a setting

of *The Lake Isle of Innisfree* on three thousand mouth organs.
His *Words for Music Perhaps* implies perhaps not. In the late
1930s he presided over a series of radio programmes intended to
demonstrate the possibilities of wedding verse to music, but his
examples were coarse and primitive, all pipe, drum and folk
song, and his harsh corncrake voice was an auditory insult. The
exquisite settings of his verses in Peter Warlock's *The Curlew*
meant nothing to him.

Popular writers, especially novelists, have felt free to exhibit
the crassest musical ignorance, though they would never dare to
commit solecisms when describing a carburettor or even a painting. Margaret Kennedy's *The Constant Nymph*, a novel of immense popularity in its day, introduced the stereotype of the
romantic composer, Lewis Dodd, a tyrant to orchestral players
('Get rid of that second violinist at the end of the row – he's a
fool') and a devil with women. He composes a great work called
Symphony in Three Keys and, to this day, one wonders whether
the work is polytonal or a mere suite without a tonal centre. A
novel about a novelist or a painter is expected to show the nature
of the artist's talent in a summary of one of his plots or an
account of the process of his working on a landscape, but the
composer–hero is immune from the reader's inspection. Bluff
can sometimes be called, however, as it is called all the time in
the Fellini film about an orchestral rehearsal, where none of the
string players use vibrato. In one story by Ethel Mannin an
orchestral composer states that the basis of the ensemble is the
pianoforte, and in another a solo violinist plays a Chopin fugue
before embarking on his own *Dream of a Summer Dawn*, which
filled listening Emily with gelatinous happiness, as though the
notes were beckoning her to embrace a joy that had hitherto only
shone fitfully in her moments of waking, etc., etc.

The two most notable fictionalizations of a musical career are
Romain Rolland's *Jean Christophe*, which deals at over-great
length with a kind of Gallicized Beethoven, and Thomas Mann's
Doctor Faustus, where musical genius is not merely close to the
id (that is why Freud distrusted music) but is an emanation of
power diabolically bestowed. We never learn exactly what Adrian
Leverkühn's music sounds like, though we suspect the Gersh-
winian worst when told that a climactic chord in his Violin

Concerto is an augmented dominant thirteenth. Rolland did not dare, despite the size of his concept, to write out the odd musical theme. Novels about composers should contain programme notes with ample illustrations. If novelists are shy about providing these, we are inclined to suspect the endowment of their genius heroes. Still, *Doctor Faustus*, despite everything, convinces. In presenting the mechanics of Leverkühn's craft, Mann commits not even a minimal error. The novel reminds us that we are long past the Johnsonian nonsense and that music and literature have a great deal to say to each other.

Among twentieth-century poets, T. S. Eliot has exhibited concern about the relationship of his own art to that of music, though commentators on his work tend to look for the wrong things when considering the quasi-musical structure of *Four Quartets*. I had read the component poems of this volume in pamphlet form before the unifying title was announced. When I first saw this title in an American periodical I misread it as *Four Quarters*, which still seems to me more apt (the whole work is about going back to places located on maps or by compass) than the one finally fixed upon. In what way are these four long meditative poems quartets? In that they have an intimacy of tone comparable to chamber music (Joyce's musical title for his volume of lyrics qualified a similar comparison by means of a coarsely ironic connotation), in that they possess a common structure analogous to the movements of late Beethovenian sonatas, whether for piano or strings, the title will do, but it is far more fanciful than the one Huxley used for an early novel – *Point Counter Point*. Huxley was attempting a fictional structure in which all the many strands of narrative were of equal importance. In a song, or even a sonata, one musical strand predominates, and all the rest is accompaniment. In the average novel there is a hero or heroine, and his or her adventures stand in a stronger light than those of other characters, whom we must term subsidiary. A work of counterpoint grants equal importance to all its linear components, and Huxley's exact structural analogy justifies the title. *Four Quartets* is too whimsical a name for the greatest meditative verse of our age.

The true musicality of Eliot is to be found elsewhere. *The Waste Land* is, among other things, a collage of literary citations,

but the purely literary approach to the work discounts the musical associations from which some of the borrowed lines cannot
well be separated. To find in the opening lines about April being
the cruellest month a verbal analogy to the opening of Stravinsky's *Sacre du Printemps* may seem over-arbitrary, but those of
us who, in Manchester in 1937, presented *The Waste Land* as
melodrama, could not evade that opening on a high solo bassoon,
and, late in life, Eliot confessed to having had that sound in
mind when writing his own opening. As the poem proceeds,
scraps of Wagner's verse appear, in the original German or in
parodic English, and Wagner's music has to go with them. After
the coffee-drinking scene, in which a reminiscence of King Ludwig appears in the form of a song – 'In the mountains, there you
feel free' – and Ludwig, who died by drowning, foreshadows
both Ophelia and Phlebas the Phoenician, we are led to the
composer of whom Ludwig was the patron:

> *Frisch weht der Wind*
> *Der Heimat zu.*
> *Mein Irisch Kind,*
> *Wo weilest du?*

This is the song sung by the sailor looking for landfall at the
beginning of *Tristan und Isolde*. It precedes the scene in the
hyacinth garden, where the wet hair and flower-filled arms of the
hyacinth girl are rejected by one of the male narrators (who, the
notes to the poem tell us, are all the same narrator). It symbolizes
ambiguously both love and sterility, because we know of the
frustrated passion of Tristan and his uncle's destined bride, and
the line that comes after the hyacinths confirms the tragedy of
love doomed. '*Oed' und leer das Meer*'. Isolde sings that phrase
shortly before the end of the third act. A whole evening of opera
is compressed into a few lines.

Eliot calls on popular song as well as Wagnerian music drama.
In the second section of the poem, 'A Game of Chess', the male
narrator sings 'O O O O that Shakespeherian Rag – It's so elegant,
so intelligent.' We need the tune for its banality:

It contradicts the Keatsian but sterile opulence of the Belladonna who is Lady of the Rocks. When her plebeian counterpart or *semblable, sa soeur*, is seduced in the middle section of the poem, the sordor of the event infects Wagner as Shakespeare has already been infected, and the three Thames daughters have to be heard as a record on the gramophone which, mingling with the whining of a mandoline, becomes a jazzed or ragged version of the song of the Rhine daughters:

In the same section another music drama of Wagner, *Parsifal*, is brought into a naked encounter with more banality. To the tune of 'Pretty Redwing' we hear about a woman who, though perhaps as plebeian as the Lil of the earlier pub conversation, is as much in contact with water as Ophelia, King Ludwig or Phlebas:

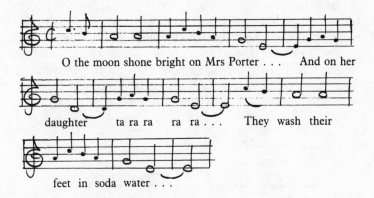

(Eliot and I have alike forgotten the phrase where I have placed ta ra ra.) Immediately after this we have Nerval's reference to the Amen sung by the *voix d'enfants, chantant dans la coupole* in *Parsifal* at the point where the washing of feet is high ceremony. We are, I think, intended to remember that Amen:

It is the inevitable background sound to the final 'Shantih shantih shantih' of the poem, another collocation of East and West which, like the end of 'The Fire Sermon', is 'not an accident'.

The musical connotations of certain phrases in *The Waste Land* may, if we wish, be ignored, but it is not possible to ignore the jazz elements in the fragment called *Sweeney Agonistes*. Eliot said in one of his essays that modern poetry could not afford to neglect the rhythms of the internal combustion engine, and he might have said the same thing about the jagged beat of popular music. This piece of an unfinished 'Aristophanic melodrama' calls, in its very subtitle, for continuous background music, even if supplied only by a side drum with wire brushes. What Eliot has recognized as the innovatory feature of jazz is syncopation, which is an aspect of its honesty. For the rhythms of speech contradict the rhythms of the body, and an honest musical setting of speech fights against regularity of accent. The sung element of jazz is far closer to speech than the stylized intonations of the *Lied*, and very frequently it is no more than speech with a slight exaggeration of the syncopated properties of speech. Thus, Eliot's Doris and Dusty speak verse which rhymes and has a regular four-beat bass pulsing beneath it (in the imagination or on a soft drum), but it is no way artificial, for there is no artificiality in the jazz from which it derives:

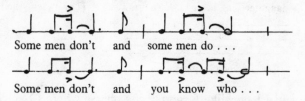

The accents of natural speech are always a little ahead of the regular beats of the heart. When Eliot gives us, in the *Fragment of an Agon*, some specimens of popular song, the syncopation which has characterized the dialogue is, in whatever setting, inevitably transferred to the notes. The following setting is my own:

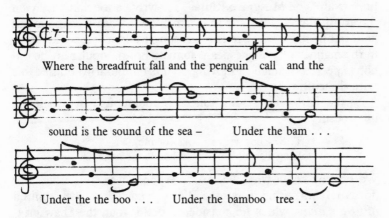

Where the breadfruit fall and the penguin call and the sound is the sound of the sea – Under the bam . . . Under the the boo . . . Under the bamboo tree . . .

It is typical of Eliot that, even in a piece of banality, he has to find the justification of an existing text. The refrain of the song comes from one sung by Lilian Russell in New York in the 1890s.

The originality of *Sweeney Agonistes* is quite considerable. To present not only a theology but a vision of hell and a rejection of redemption in the rhythms of jazz is a large literary achievement, and yet nowhere, except in the title, subtitles and epigraphs, is there an evocation of literature. The materials are commonplace and the speech crude but the effect is devastating. The work is presented as an 'unfinished poem', and it is a pity that Eliot did not seem able to pursue this new technique in a completed large-scale dramatic work. But there was always a 'double standard' in Eliot's approach to popular art which forbade a serious synthesis of the high and the low. He was something of a rogue, said Edmund Wilson, but not perhaps enough of one. He flirted with the entertainments of the common people but then grew scared and ran away.

He was always promising to attempt a serious critical evaluation of the detective story, but he probably failed, as he did in his essay on Kipling, to find the right tools for dissecting what, being merely good, was the enemy of the best. He admired Conan Doyle's Sherlock Holmes stories but did not see how they could be literature. And yet, at the most solemn moment of the first scene of *Murder in the Cathedral*, he lifts, verbatim, some lines from 'The Musgrave Ritual'. He wrote a touching essay on the art of Marie Lloyd and in it lamented the death of the music hall, but he knew that a music-hall song could never be literature in the manner of a Shakespeare sonnet. From popular art he did not expect too much. Enjoying it, he temporarily doused his critical faculties.

Eartha Kitt sang a song called 'Monotonous', in which the lines occur

> T. S. Eliot writes books for me,
> King Farouk's on tenterhooks for me.

We do not know what Farouk's response was, but Eliot sent flowers. It was timid flirtation. Eliot is reported to have admired *My Fair Lady*, which he considered better than the Shaw original. This means that he admired stupidities like

> Arabians learn Arabian with the speed of summer lightning,
> And Hebrews learn it backwards, which is really rather frightening

and solecisms (which Shaw would never have permitted) like

> I'd be equally as willing
> For a dentist to be drilling
> Than to ever let a woman in my life.

Words sung, we must remember, by a self-appointed guardian of correct English. To Eliot, however, the double standard permitted acceptance in demotic art of what would have been anathema in the true literary tradition.

And yet Eliot was the one poet and critic of the age who was qualified to recognize that certain reaches of popular art protected traditions of craftsmanship, intelligence, wit and taste that artists acclaimed by the intelligentsia had abandoned. Philip Larkin, a very considerable poet as well as a serious student of jazz, recently stated that his literary ambitions were first fired by certain popular songs of the 1930s. This 'middle eight' of 'Love is just around the corner', for instance:

> Venus de Milo was noted for her charms.
> Strictly between us,
> You're cuter than Venus
> And, what's more, you've got arms.

He might also have cited this, from 'Mamma, I wanna make rhythm':

> I have no desire to carry a S-
> -tradivarious,
> But there's no limit of
> Primitive
> Tom-tom in my tum-tum.

Brash, yes, but not crude. Witty, but not rarefied. And exemplifying the possibility of a perfect marriage between colloquial speech rhythms and the rhythms of music.

The evaluation of the lyric – meaning words not for silent reading nor even public recitation but for fitting to music – has been too much in the hands of the men of letters. I read recently in a new book on Shakespeare's poetic achievement that the dirge in *Cymbeline* ('Fear no more the heat o' the sun') was the best lyric ever written. But what are the grounds for such a judgement? There have been several musical settings, but none are memorable. It has not inspired a distinguished melody. It is thought of not as a song but as a number of stanzas on a page. It is only when words can be freed from the page, and from their formal lineation on it, that we may start to discuss lyric excellence.

Yeats is considered to be a lyric giant, while his compatriot Thomas Moore is regarded as a mere minor versifier, but the admirable brief poems of *The Tower* and *The Winding Stair*, though they sometimes have refrains in the manner of a song, have nothing to do with the lyric craft. Moore's superiority as a writer of lyrics is attested by the inferiority of his *Irish Melodies* as poetry. Poetry demands the concentration of the reader or listener on content, on originality of imagery or verbal trope; the true lyric deliberately damps the striking image, graciously obscuring the light of the words so as to affirm a true marriage of equal partners. Moore did what all accomplished lyrists do: he took an existing melody and attached words to it. He knew that a melody already possesses *in potentia* the pattern of a literal infinitude of verbal constructs. The skill lies in recognition of the nature of this pattern and the choice of a verbal statement which clarifies it. What is said is not of great importance.

In a lyric like 'Believe me, if all those endearing young charms', we would be unwise to look for those verbal shocks which confirm the presence of great poetry. The poetry here dare not be great; the images, though neat and appropriate, must not obtrude. What is important is the matching of long vowels or diphthongs to long notes, the disposition of primary and secondary syllabic stress, and the management of climax. Melody is made out of internal repetition, and the whole construct is itself repeated, sometimes more than once. The skill of Moore is heard in the repetitions, where the interest and imagery of the verbal discourse mount, though never too much, and the challenge of a musical climax is met in a way corresponding in emotional intensity, but rarely in verbal form, to the first statement:

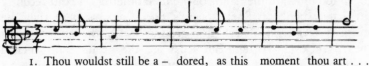

1. Thou wouldst still be a – dored, as this   moment thou art . . .
2. But   the   heart that has   tru – ly   loved ne –ver for – gets . . .

Here the second syllable of the participle 'adored' and the first syllable of the adverb 'truly' carry exactly the same weight of musical, and hence emotional, intensity. On the printed page 'truly' seems conventional and otiose, but it is revealed as both fresh and inevitable when sung.

There is in Moore's lyrical language a great deal that is conventional and, even in his own time, had the quality of an artificial flower: there was a potential seediness suitable for Joxer Daly and the Paycock. Some of the images are merely gallant – 'As the sunflower turns on her god as he sets/The same look that she turned when he rose' – though others are capable of mild wit:

> The sage's glass we'll shun, my dear,
> For, catching the flight
> Of bodies of light,
> He may happen to take thee for one, my dear.

But the excellence of his verses as lyrics has little to do with what we expect from literature. The drawing rooms of London were charmed by the tenor of the leprechaun at the keyboard, but Ireland treated Moore as a hero. Song-writers are rarer than poets, and song-writers who can articulate a national feeling, as Moore did, are rarest of all.

The lyrist who nearest approached Moore in our own century had none of Moore's qualities except technical skill. Lorenz Hart was American Jewish of German descent, claiming a relationship to Heinrich Heine, depressed, alcoholic, homosexual, under-sized, given to none of the high, if formal, sentiments of Moore, very much a New Yorker oscillating between the cynical and the sentimental. He was more concerned with heightening the spoken word than with finding a melodic justification for conventional romantic statements in a received pseudo-poetic form. He worked with Richard Rodgers in a number of Broadway musicals before drink, despair and early death capped his fountain pen for good, and then Rodgers collaborated with Oscar Hammerstein II. Reading Rodgers's autobiography, one is astonished to find the composer apparently unaware of the aesthetic gulf between the two lyrists. Hammerstein was competent but never brilliant. In the first Rodgers–Hart song to become popular, 'Manhattan', these lines appear:

> Our future babies
> We'll take to 'Abie's
> Irish Rose'.
> We hope they live to see it close.

A recent redaction, assuming that 'Abie's Irish Rose' has been long forgotten, substitutes

> And 'South Pacific'
> Is a terrific
> Show, they say.
> We'll have to take it in some day

There is an unkind cut. It puts into the mouth of a lyrist all too prone to depression an acceptance of the popular, and untenable, view of the talent of the man who succeeded him. A ventriloquial tribute from the urn of ashes.

It is not my intention to examine Hart's lyrics in any depth, merely to say something about their prosody. They rhyme well, sometimes conventionally, sometimes ingeniously, and they rhyme as often as they can:

> We'll have Manhattan,
> The Bronx and Staten
> Island too.
> It's lovely going through
> The Zoo.

The effect is of a very natural conversational declaration which, by the happiest of accidents, has rhymes in it.

> Beans would get no keener re-
> ception in a beanery.
> Bless our mountain greenery home.

The ingenious rhyme does not seem forced. And, without forcing, Hart manages to find rhymes lying around even in colourless morphemes:

> Not a lot of
> Just a plot of
> Land
> And
> Thou swell, thou pretty, thou grand.

I have transcribed these lyrical scraps, held in memory, in the form most readers of verse expect. Such a form makes the rhyme of 'keener re-' and 'beanery' seems whimsical and over-contrived. The eye has traditionally had far too much to say about what constitutes an acceptable rhyme, and rhyming dictionaries (one of which I confess shamelessly to have, in the throes of lyricizing for Broadway, lavishly used) assume that only lexemes, or autosemantemes, or words with space before and after, are permitted to rhyme. This is an ocular convention, and it is responsible for the fallacy that certain words have no rhymes or at most very few. 'Fugue' is said to have no rhyme, but in a Hart-type lyric it could have more than one:

> A concert, Hugo?
> By all means *you* go,
> But the very first note of a fugue o-
> presses me, like all polyphony.
> I'd sooner have a diamond from Tiffany.

'Love', traditionally chained to 'above' and 'dove', has more choice in the lyric covenant:

> God knows I've tried
> To make my shovel shove
> A rubble of
> Irrecoverable love aside.

The complex rhyme did not, of course, begin with Lorenz Hart. We find it in Robert Browning, who was a musician, and W. S. Gilbert, who wrote words for music, and also in Thomas Hood and in Barham's *Ingoldsby Legends*, but the Victorian intention was more heavily comic than witty: the grotesque rhyme was a signal that the rules of seriousness were being broken. With Hart and his followers there is a certain ambiguity of feeling, wit in the service of frustration or neurosis, and the rhymes do not really call attention to themselves, even at their most ingenious:

> Take off the gloomy mask of tragedy:
> It's not your style.
> Take off and zoom. Now aren't you glad you de-
> cided to smile?

That is from 'Bye Bye Birdie', and I have forgotten the identity of the lyrist. This accords with a certain self-effacement in the Broadway genre. We are not dealing with egotistical romantic poets but with skilled craftsmen serving stars.

This concern with rhymes is not so superficial as it appears. A rhyme is a witty thing in itself, if by wit we mean the reconciliation of disparities in the smallest possible form. In his *Little Night Music*, Stephen Sondheim, perhaps Hart's true successor and a composer himself, sums up the tedium of prolonged Scandinavian summer light in a tiny rhyme –

> Let the hands of the clock turn
> But don't sing a nocturne
> Yet

– and, like any true poet, fixes in one's skull for ever a truth expressed in a verbal inevitability. For it is the inevitability of

the rhyme that conditions the wit, and inevitability is not something we find in Browning's

> While treading down rose and ranunculus
> You Tommy-make-room-for-your-uncle us.

In transcribing the above lyric phrases in conventional verse
notation, I am obscuring a major formal difference between the
song lyric and the independent poem. The shape of the song
lyric is determined by a musical pattern, even when there is as
yet no music for it: consider, say, 'Go and catch a falling star' in
Donne's *Songs and Sonnets*. Its rhymes, while serving the end of
wit in the widest sense of the term – unity in diversity and
diversity in unity – are a verbal acknowledgement of the presence
of musical nodes – points of rest, significant repetitions, ca-
dences. Consequently it is not in order to speak of end or internal
rhymes, since a song does not end till its last bar and hence all
its rhymes except the last are internal. Or, put it another way,
there are no lines in lyric verse: there are only paragraphs containing verbal phrases that correspond to musical phrases. To
read a piece of music is to see the representation of a continuous
statement whose verbal equivalent would not be verse but prose
– though a prose without paragraph indentations. The words of
a song are set down continuously and without lineal break. There
are no spaces to facilitate recognition of forms, such as the sonnet
or ottava rima or whatever ad hoc pattern is imposed by the
music. This expresses not a limitation, in comparison with the
written or printed form of conventional verse, but rather an
advantage, since there is no possibility of the ocular seduction
which suggests verse when there is none, and we are forced into
the salutary position of deciding what verse really is.

Most prosodists take it for granted that the unit of verse is the
line, but what sonic validity does the line possess? Take the
following:

> April is the cruellest month, breeding
> Lilacs out of the dead land, mixing
> Memory and desire, stirring
> Dull roots with spring rain.
> Winter kept us warm, covering

>   Earth in forgetful snow, feeding
>   A little life with dried tubers.

Eliot is making what is evidently a poetic statement. He is not
addressing the brain, as with an official directive, and demanding
the response of action. A complex message is being delivered to
the imagination, and its semiotic elements include an exploitation
of the sound of words that would be irrelevant, or even harmful,
in a piece of didactic writing. There are five present participles,
and their identical endings provide a sonic pattern that does not
relate to lexical meaning. Poetry, without a doubt, but is it verse?
It is assumed to be verse because of its lineal setting, but, set
continuously like prose, it would still be poetry. The placing of
the like endings at the end of lines does not impose a method of
oral delivery, real or imagined. There is not, as there has to be
in music, any *structural* significance in the notation.

This is, admittedly, free verse, and free verse presents prosodic
problems which no one really wishes to solve. But with traditional regular patterns – or rather with one such pattern – the
line takes on a meaning because it is the equivalent of a musical
measure. I mean the four-beat line or tetrameter:

>   Had we but world enough and time
>   This coyness, lady, were no crime.

We *have* time, and it is common time, the four-crotchet-to-a-bar
beat which, so it is said, comes closest to the pulse of nature.
Now the metre of the heart beat, or of walking, is duple, not
quadruple, and common time, or the line of four accents, has to
be regarded as a cultural structure which subtly varies the beat
of nature. The four-beat line or bar begins with a strong accent
and the accents which follow progressively decay. With each
fresh bar or line there is a recovery of strength at the beginning,
and then progressive weakening, and the process continues
throughout the whole musical, or verse, structure. This means
that rhyme comes at the weakest point of the line.

Set those two lines of Andrew Marvell to music, and we could
have something like this:

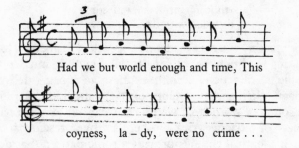

This is not typical of song, where rhymes are rarely associated with weak beats (or up-beats), but the mere attempt to set the lines discloses why four-beat rhyming couplets always seem to possess a quality of non-assertiveness and are suitable for gallantry or pastoral. The rhyme is not hammered out; it is almost thrown away. This is not true of five-beat rhyming lines, or heroic couplets:

> Know then thyself, presume not God to scan:
> The proper study of mankind is man.

Yet, logically, a fifth beat should be even weaker than a fourth. This, however, is only if we are prepared to accept five-four time, five crotchets to the bar, as a natural measure, and few of us are able to do that. Five to a bar contradicts the duple beat of nature, and if we are willing to take it in music this is because the music itself seems to be a denial of nature. The first movement of Holst's *Planets* is in five-four time, sometimes augmenting itself to five-two, and it represents Mars, the bringer of war. The regular common time of a military march might have seemed appropriate to a composer writing in the time of Napoleon, but Holst is aware that machines have taken over from marching feet, and these machines are in the service of destruction – a monstrous denial of life, or nature. His final movement – 'Neptune, the Mystic' – is in a slower five-four, and this again is fitting for the transcendence of nature, an assertion of a reality beyond the rhythms of the earth. We can accept also the five-beat intermezzo of Tchaikovsky's Sixth Symphony, where there is a kind of neurotic charm in a failed attempt to adjust to nature: the composer does not know whether he wants a three-four or a two-four dance measure, and he gives us both. But to accept a five-beat line as a basic English verse measure seems an inexcusable eccentricity, yet English poets have done this ever since Chaucer.

They have done it because of the influence of an alien culture – that of the French, which was also a way into Italian culture – whose language, and hence whose poetry, did not depend for its prosodic patterns on principles of stress. English, like all the Germanic tongues, is heavily stressed, and its verse forms in Anglo-Saxon and early Middle English poetry came close to music in accepting accent as the basis of rhythm. With the Norman influence the syllabic principle was imposed, against the nature of English. In a French alexandrine the counting of six stresses means less than the counting of twelve syllables, and there is no relationship between the verse line and the musical bar. We can trace this prosodic system back to the example of classical verse. In reading Homer or Virgil we have to invoke 'quantity' – syllabic length, not stress – and we are a world away from the powerful recurrent beats, reinforced with head-rhyme, which we find in Anglo-Saxon poetry and which, in *Ulysses*, Joyce expertly parodied: 'Loud on left Thor thundered: in anger awful the hammerhurler.'

Terms like iambic pentameter and trochaic tetrameter and dactylic dimeter do not fit well into systems of English prosody, where the more realistic modes of quasi-musical description ought to apply. And the pentameter has more relevance to syllabic or quantitative verse than to a poetic tradition based on common time or four in a bar. Whether we like it or not, when we hear a five-beat line we are really hearing a four-beat one followed by the first beat of a second which is not permitted to complete itself. That couplet from Pope's *Essay on Man* suggests this kind of setting (not that anyone would ever wish to set it):

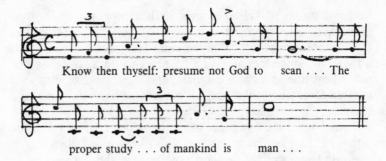

Here the bars truncated by the anomalous prosody are filled out. A modern composer would have no compunction in shortening them, so that there could be an alternation of four-four and two-four, or a single bar of three-two as the basic measure. But the nature of English, and the kinship of English verse with musical metre, forbids the acceptance of a pentameter as the verse equivalent of a bar in five-four time.

The liberation of the five-beat line from traditional rhyme schemes to become the accepted medium for Elizabethan drama has always been considered a great prosodic achievement: it brought verse as close to natural speech as was possible within the poetic confines of the genre, without sacrificing the rhetorical advantages of a lineal unit and a fixed beat. It was not a medium that the dramatists discovered for themselves: the Earl of Surrey used it in a partial translation of the *Aeneid*, hearing in the unrhymed pentameter the best native (i.e. modified Norman French) counterpart to the unrhymed hexameter of Virgil. That it is an unnatural form few have considered, and the achievements of Marlowe, Shakespeare and Ben Jonson have rendered such a consideration improper or even blasphemous.

Marlowe, indeed, saw that the 'running on' of the blank verse line into paragraphs fought against nature, and his 'mighty line', as Ben Jonson termed it, is an exploitation of the single five-beat unit, with a pause at the end that pays homage to three beats of four-four time that are registered unconsciously and unconsciously speeded up. This, for instance, from *Edward II*:

In Naples did I learn to poison flowers.

And this, from *Dr Faustus*:

> See where Christ's blood streams in the firmament.

Every line of the speech Faustus makes to Helen is 'mighty' in the sense that it bears the weight of two bars of common time:

> Was this the face that launched a thousand ships
> And burned the topless towers of Ilium?
> Sweet Helen, make me immortal with a kiss.
> Her lips suck forth my soul – see, where it flies.
> Come, Helen, come, give me my soul again . . .

Every line of the speech, and not just the third, could be followed by a kiss of a full three beats' duration.

We can best demonstrate, admittedly grotesquely, this doubly tetrametric nature (increasingly thwarted as blank verse became more 'mature', less 'end-stopt', closer to speech) by taking the four best-known lines of Shakespeare:

> To be or not to be, that is the question:
> Whether 'tis nobler in the mind to suffer
> The slings and arrows of outrageous fortune,
> Or to take arms against a sea of troubles. . .

Imagine, in some absurdist production, Hamlet speaking his lines and a chorus inserting statements of its own:

> To be or not to be, that is the
> Question. (There's a frightful cat, is there?)
> Whether 'tis nobler in the mind to
> Suffer – (Birds go mad in cages.)
> The slings and arrows of outrageous
> Fortune – (We're the caged-up kind too.)
> Or to take arms against a sea of
> Troubles (We don't have the key of.)

The weight of the fifth beat of the blank verse line is made evident in the above nonsense: it is the heavy stress of the beginning of a bar. The 'running on' process was bound, sooner or later, to break the hegemony of the line as a structural unit. If the verse line cannot be identified with the musical bar it has no significance. Here is late Shakespeare:

> And his pond fish'd by his next neighbour, by
> Sir Smile, his neighbour. . .

That is often cited as the final liberating achievement. Such liberation leads us to prose. Eliot knew this, but he did not dare say so.

I have come some distance from 'Under the bamboo tree'. The first quatrain of Omar Khayyam, the original, not Fitzgerald, describes the Cyrus of the day taking the dome of the mosque and inverting it to make a cup, so that it may be filled with the white dry wine of the dawn. The Persian word for cup is *jam*, and for dome or roof *bam*. I have been suggesting, no more, that the study of English verse ought to be housed in the halls of a wider study of rhythms and stress – be, in fact, under the *bam* of music.

7
Nothing is so Beautiful as Sprung

To Father Gerard Manley Hopkins SJ we owe a new system of prosody and a prosodic terminology that speaks not Greek but English. The following lines are the start of one of his sonnets:

Nothing is so beautiful as spring –
When weeds, in wheels, shoot long and lovely and lush.

That second line is what used to be called an iambic pentameter. It is now to be called a line of five feet with a rising rhythm. Rising means starting with an unstressed syllable and moving on to a stressed one – from, in Hopkinsian terminology, a slack to a stress. The first line has reversed feet – that is, it starts on a stressed syllable and moves to an unstressed one, and so on for all five feet, except that the final foot lacks a slack (catalectic in Greek). This is falling rhythm. Because the first line does not accord with the rising rhythmical pattern expected in a sonnet, Hopkins liked to think it was *counterpointed* to the orthodox metre, but we need not take too much notice of this. Those two lines are rhythmically not very startling, they are in pretty near total conformity with the practice of Shakespeare and Wordsworth. They employ orthodox, or near-orthodox, running rhythm. Opposed to running rhythm is sprung rhythm, which is a more complicated matter or metre.

Let us take a line not by Hopkins but by Eliot – the last line of the song 'My Little Island Girl' in *Sweeney Agonistes*:

Mórning, évening, nóontime, níght.

This is trochaic tetrameter catalectic, or, in the new terminology, a four-foot (or four-beat) line in falling rhythm. The alternation of stress and slack is traditional and expected. Suppose we now remove the slacks or unaccented syllables:

Mórn, éve, nóon, níght.

Recite the two lines and time your recitation with a stopwatch. You will find that they take exactly the same number of seconds. We have lost three syllables but duration is not affected nor is the number of stresses to the line. When we get the naked juxtaposition of stresses without the cushioning of slacks, we are in the presence of sprung rhythm. We are also in its presence when the number of syllables between stresses is augmented beyond what tradition would allow:

In the mórning, in the évening, sometimes at nóontime, nearly always at níght.

The two slacks preceding *morning* are, of course, not between stresses, unless the final stress of the previous line is to be taken into account, but, since we are taking the line as the unit, we can call the slacks before the first stress the anacrusis, as in music. The number of syllables all told is nineteen and is totally inadmissible in the old dispensation. Over some of these syllables we have to hurry so that the ear does not lose the basic beat, but that basic pattern of four stresses – on *morn, eve, noon, night* – is still there. The foot beginning on *noon* has seven syllables and, unless we rush them, we may slow down the beat. Hopkins regarded syllables which did that as somehow outside the rhythm, a legitimate slowing down as in music, and called such an overloaded foot an outride.

Sprung rhythm seems so called because the movement of the verse springs out of the element which makes it verse – namely, the isochronous recurrence of a stress. You are no longer concerned, and never should have been, with the number of syllables to the line, only with the number of stresses. We gain a startling conviction of the possibilities of sprung rhythm when we tamper with well-known lines in ordinary running rhythm.

Lét me nót to the márriage of trúe mínds

can become

Lét me néver to the mátrimony of éverloving mínds.

You have to stutter, but there are still only five stresses, and the new line takes no longer to recite than does the old. And this version takes no less time:

Lét's nót wéd úntrue mínds.

Five stresses still. Note that Shakespeare seems, in his cunning way, to be already anticipating Hopkins. His first foot has the orthodox two syllables, but the second and the third have three each, while the two final words have a foot each to themselves – stresses without the cushioning of slacks. But it is more common in English poetry than is realized to counterpoint (in Hopkins's sense) a speech rhythm to a metre – in Shakespeare's instance iambic pentameter, or a five-foot line in rising rhythm. Orthodox prosodists spoke of reversing feet. They could not permit an increase in the number of syllables, or a decrease either: Shakespeare's line has exactly ten syllables. There is a compromise between quantitative scanning (syllable-counting) and qualitative (stress-counting). With sprung rhythm the compromise is at an end: you have as few or as many syllables as you wish, so long as you cling to a pattern of stresses. A Hopkins sonnet, however hurried or slowed its syllabic content, always has the same number of stresses to the line – usually five, but sometimes six, and once even eight. Those lines behave precisely as music behaves.

Hopkins, priest, poet, naturalist, Ruskinian draughtsman, was also a musician. He composed music, none of it very good, though in his setting of Canon Dixon's 'Falling Rain' he demonstrated a sharpness of ear which enabled him to distinguish microtones: he anticipated Hába of the twentieth century by finding a notation for half-flats and half-sharps. The melody of 'Falling Rain' is not in itself daring enough to justify division of the semitone. Dutifully I have given the song the piano accompaniment Hopkins was not skilled enough to provide himself, but nothing can disguise the amateurishness of the melodic datum. All of Hopkins's songs were performed recently in a special concert broadcast by the radio station at Anchorage, Alaska: they made little impact on the snowbound musical. (Curious that history should have chosen the wrong one of the two most recent United States: Hawaii would have been more fitting: Hopkins's father was consul-general there and wrote a history of the islands.)

Hopkins was in much the same musical situation as Bernard Shaw, who knew all about music but could not compose it and had to be satisfied with musicalizing his true art. Shaw's plays contain arias, ensembles and cadenzas, and they insist on exploiting the vocal spectrum, so that each play has its soprano, tenor, baritone, basso cantante and so on. Hopkins treated the poetic art as if it were music, and his prosodic system demonstrated the rhythmical kinship between the two arts. He did more: he made the rhetoric of his poetry approach music in its imitation of dynamics and significant pauses, and he seemed to be working towards a contrapuntalization of verbal language which it was left to James Joyce to fulfil.

In December 1875, when Hopkins was towards the end of his Jesuit novitiate, the passenger ship *Deutschland*, American-outward-bound from Bremen, was wrecked at the mouth of the Thames. Among the drowned were five Franciscan nuns, exiled from Germany under the Falck laws, which forbade that education should be in the hands of religious orders. Hopkins's rector expressed a wish that someone should write a poem on the disaster. Hopkins had already written a good deal of verse, much of it of a strong Pre-Raphaelite cast, but, believing that pleasure in art conflicted with his priestly vocation, he had destroyed most of his poems. Now granted an imprimatur on the resumption of his craft, he wrote *The Wreck of the Deutschland*. During his poetic silence his ear, he said, had been 'haunted by a new rhythm'. This owed something to 'certain chimes suggested by the Welsh poetry I had been reading (what they call the *cynghanedd*).' It was at St Beuno's, 'on a pastoral forehead in Wales', that the poem was written. It was offered to the Jesuit magazine *The Month*, but it was rejected as odd and not easily intelligible.

The poem *is* obscure, and I may tentatively offer a principle which partially explains obscurity in all literature – the desire of the writer to come close to music. For if we take in verbal constructs primarily as sound and structure without a clearly separable meaning, then we are much in the position of listening to music. Hopkins is never unintelligible: his urgent need to say something forbids the linguistic play of surrealism, which we may identify for the Victorian age with the Learian self-indulgence of nonsense. But his very concern with exactness of expression leads him to the choice of little-known words or the fashioning of neologisms. The conflict in his very complex personality between Christian asceticism and native sensuousness sometimes makes for ambiguity. His impatience with words which, having a purely structural function, lack semantic content results frequently in ellipsis and difficult syntax. He had both the poetic and the missionary urge to present a theological concept in a flavoursome sensuous brevity: he had to compress his thought and feeling into small entities of great mass – even when granting himself the width of the ode, as in *The Wreck of the Deutschland*. The musical analogies are obvious. Language distinguishes between the autosemanteme (or word containing meaning) and the synsemanteme (the morpheme which assists in the making of meaning but has no meaning in itself), but in music all units are meaningful: there is nothing that is purely structural. Music deals in sounds without clear referents. Music is multiguous, since it is capable of many interpretations. Music, one might say, is Hopkinsian.

Consider the situation of a complex poetic mind like that of Hopkins faced with the task of composing *The Wreck of the Deutschland*. This is to be no mere 'Toll for the brave'. The shipwreck is real and apt for the reports of *The Times* (which Hopkins read), but it is also symbolic. *Deutschland* is 'double a desperate name': it is the name of a ship but also of a country which reared the Lutheran heresy and has learned religious intolerance. The storm which wrecks the ship is in the human mind, in history, as well as raging round the Kentish Knock. There is Hopkins's own storm to consider: the spiritual struggle which led to his conversion, the alienation of family and friends. There is the theme of sacrifice. Nothing available in the poetic canon of the time, not Tennyson nor Browning nor Matthew Arnold, could provide fitting language or form. The art of Protestant Victorian England was, in general, of a blandness that forbade the shocks administered by Donne and Shakespeare in words and Gesualdo in music. But there were shocks enough in the 'music of the future' to which concert-going England shut its ears. Less than six months after the wreck of the *Deutschland*, Shaw was welcoming the 'apostle' of this music to England, with his 'one hundred and ten strings in all; six flutes, six oboes, two *corni inglesi*, six clarinets, one bass clarinet, six bassoons, one *contrafagotto*, eight horns, six trumpets, four trombones, four tubas, one contra-bass tuba, two pairs of kettle-drums, one triangle, one pair of cymbals, one side drum, one glockenspiel, and six harps. Surely, since King Nebuchadnezzar set up the golden image, no such an assemblage of musical instruments was ever collected together.' This was not a Tennysonian or even Browningian music, but it was certainly Hopkinsian. Yet did Hopkins ever hear Wagner?

We can find, in the literature of 1877, no analogue to *The Wreck of the Deutschland*. Its effects are Wagnerian:

> Well, she has thee for the pain, for the
> Patience; but pity of the rest of them!
> Heart, go and bleed at a bitterer vein for the
> Comfortless unconfessed of them –
> No, not uncomforted: lovely-felicitous Providence
> Finger of a tender of, O of a feathery delicacy, the breast of the
> Maiden could obey so, be a bell to, ring of it, and
> Startle the poor sheep back! is the shipwrack then a harvest, does
> tempest carry the grain for thee?

Here is sprung rhythm in action, and it can sometimes be as difficult to read as a modern orchestral (post-Wagnerian) score. The last line is a hexameter, or six-beat line, and it is hard not merely to utter within the framework of the stresses: it is hard to discover where the stresses fall. (Try *Startle the poor* as an anacrusis, then put the accents on *sheep, ship, harv, temp, car, grain.*) The line has lost its old status as a verse unit, since the rhymes insist on overrunning, enforcing the reading of the whole stanza as a paragraph almost without pause to take in breath. *Providence* rhymes with *of it and s-*, and it would be a comic effect in Browning, but the eccentricity here is swallowed up in the urgency of the total statement. (*Grain for thee* clearly does not rhyme with *pain, for the* and *vein for the*, unless an Irvingesque or Gladstonian *schwa* is substituted for an orthodox /i:/.) Here we see the first of the problems of sprung rhythm – the lack of a suitable notation. For the traditional verse setting which is good enough for Tennyson is not good enough for Hopkins.

Hopkins attempted, in the manuscript of *Harry Ploughman*, which Robert Bridges reproduced in the first, 1918, edition of the poems, to provide an idiosyncratic but unequivocal mode of presenting that sonnet in a kind of hybrid score – neither true music nor true verse – but generally he had to be content with indicating stress through diacritics. Not even these have gone down well with his readers, who tend to misread them or ignore them. Hopkins, in fact, is read too much and recited too little, yet he insisted on the primacy of the auditory experience. Of his other wreck poem, *The Loss of the Eurydice*, he wrote to Bridges: 'To do the *Eurydice* any kind of justice you must not slovenly read it with the eyes but with your ears, as if the paper were declaiming it at you.' And again: 'Indeed when, on somebody returning me the *Eurydice*, I opened and read some lines, reading, as one commonly reads whether prose or verse, with the eyes, so to say, only, it struck me aghast with a kind of raw nakedness and unmitigated violence I was unprepared for: but take breath and read with the ears, as I always wish to be read, and my verse becomes all right.' If *The Loss of the Eurydice* is easier to read, either with eyes or ears, than *The Wreck of the Deutschland*, it is because it is composed in a simpler pattern in which the sprung rhythm is more clearly perceived, or heard.

Here, in that poem, is Hopkins dealing in masterly fashion with storm and rhyme:

> A beetling baldbright cloud through England
> Riding: there did storms not mingle? and
>   Hailropes hustle and grind their
> Heavengravel? wolfsnow, worlds of it, wind there?

We know where we stand here, as we do not always in the intricately structured stanza of the greater poem. Four stresses to three lines and three to one: we are close to the basic patterns of music: the clarity of the stresses enables us to take in the four-syllabled foot that begins the last line with no trouble. We may even accept the elliptical syntax:

> But to Christ lord of thunder
> Crouch; lay knee by earth low under:

'Holiest, loveliest, bravest,
Save my hero, O Hero savest.'

The relative pronoun is too colourless for Hopkins, and without historical precedent, though with good analogical arguments ('the money I lost'), he omits it. Emboldened, he will soon be ready for the last stanza of *The Bugler's First Communion*:

Recorded only, I have put my lips on pleas
Would brandle adamantine heaven with ride and jar, did
Prayer go disregarded:
Forward-like, but however, and like favourable heaven heard these.

Here there are, in the last line, several colourless particles; brooding on them, looking for a structure, we blow their dead greyness into a flame, but it is not a flame of meaning.

Hopkins considered *The Windhover* 'the best thing I ever wrote'. It merits our close examination now as the classic deployment of his innovations.

I caught this morning morning's minion, king-
dom of daylight's dauphin, dapple-dawn-drawn falcon, in his riding
Of the rolling level underneath him steady air, and striding
High there, how he rung upon the rein of a wimpling wing
In his ecstasy! then off, off forth on swing,
As a skate's heel sweeps smooth on a bow-bend: the hurl and gliding
Rebuffed the big wind. My heart in hiding
Stirred for a bird, – the achieve of, the mastery of the thing!

Brute beauty and valour and act, oh, air, pride, plume, here
Buckle! AND the fire that breaks from thee then, a billion
Times told lovelier, more dangerous, O my chevalier!

No wonder of it: shèer plòd makes plough down sillion
Shine, and blue-bleak embers, ah my dear,
Fall, gall themselves, and gash gold-vermilion.

The first line is metrically orthodox, lulling the reader into an expectation of five-beat rising running rhythm throughout, but the breaking of the final word warns us to be ready for other breakages. As always with a five-foot line, there is awkwardness in the running over of syntax; how much more so with the fracturing of a semanteme. We want to pause on *king-*, and we are probably expected to: the pause places *minion* and *king* in apposition for a moment, and the identification will seem absurd

– the king is also the king's favourite or darling – until we remember that Hopkins's dedication of the poem is to 'Christ our Lord', and theology puts everything right. The kingdom belongs to the prince or dauphin; God the Father is king and his Son necessarily prince, but the doctrine of the Trinity presents a mystery which contradicts any purely human hierarchy.

In the second line the problems of sprung rhythm are upon us. The stresses have to fall on *day, dauph, dap, falc, rid*, and this necessitates a hurrying over *dapple-dawn-drawn* which neutralizes what is both a cliché and an internal rhyme of little value: the compound epithet is thrown away, a near-empty formula on the surface but, as pure glossolalia, expressive of the speed of flight. With the third line the unwary reader will wish to import the rhythm of six stresses (often a great temptation with the more packed of Hopkins's five-beat lines) but he must take breath and place the accents on *roll, lev, neath, stead* and *strid*. The fourth line presents another hexametric temptation, but, giving the first foot four syllables, the second foot the same, and the third three syllables, the reader finds himself on known ground, or air, with *wimpling wing* – orthodox falling rhythm. The rest of the octave should offer no difficulties. Note the contrast in movement between lines 5 and 6 – the first very hurried, the second very slow, with accents on *big* and *wind*. The *stirred/bird* rhyme is a little banal, but Hopkins always takes advantage of what chimes the language naturally offers, whether at the head or the end of a word. This is a means of underlining stress (as with *daylight's dauphin, dapple-, steady/striding, rung/rein, wimpling wing*, etc.) and, to the studious reader, it is bound to recall the practice of Anglo-Saxon verse mingled with *cynghanedd*. There is perhaps another reason, but I shall come to this later.

In the sestet Hopkins helps us to read the rhythm, by capitalizing a conjunction and providing a pair of diacritics, but it is typical of him to grant aid where we least need it and withhold it where we cry out for it. In the first line *Brute* has to be an anacrusis before the down-beat, but it is a stressed anacrusis belonging to no line and classifiable as an outride. The accents of the line fall on *beaut, val, act, air* and *here*, but the phrase *air, pride, plume* properly calls for less hurry than the rhythm enforces. We can slow down and think in terms of an outride, but two outrides in one line are too much. In the following line I have always felt the strong stress on *AND* to be forced and in the service of no special meaning. I should have preferred to scan the line, in terms of the sense, rather differently, but Fr Hopkins is in charge. The foot beginning with *breaks* has five syllables. The temptation to scan the line hexametrically, with a caesura after *fire*, is very powerful. The third line of the first tercet demands a stress on *O*. The penultimate line of the whole poem is in traditional running rhythm. Partly this is, by invoking traditional metrical practice, to prepare us for a citation from a poet who worked in that tradition. In George Herbert's *Love* the soul says to Christ: 'I the unkind, ungentle? Ah my dear/I cannot look on thee.' The heart in hiding is doubly stirred – by Christ's beauty as symbolized in the kestrel's flight, by awareness of its own imperfection. The soul cannot achieve the beauty of the Creator–Redeemer, but it can engage itself in humble service, like a plough or a kitchen fire. The steel of the ploughman sheerly plodding gives off silver light and the falling dying coals give off a flash of royal colour. These revelations just happen, as the beauty of the windhover happens, without fanfares: 'No wonder of it'.

It is not within my present brief to explicate this sonnet, but form and content are, as always in a great artist, one thing, and if I find this poem approaches the condition of music I must find a relationship between its sound and the poet's imaginative intention. That *The Windhover* is complex and even ambiguous has often been said by literary critics, and one particular word has been taken to be the focus of its complexity and ambiguity. This is *buckle* in line 9. In his *Seven Types of Ambiguity* Professor Empson found here the seventh and most difficult type, when a word means two totally opposed things. Hopkins uses *buckle* in the sense of fastening, as of a belt before military action, and in the sense of collapsing, as of a bicycle wheel. The attributes of the kestrel, or Christ our Lord, are seen as a unity in a single flash of perception. The brute beauty is purified into an almost heraldic elegance, emphasized by the courtly terms of French origin – *dauphin, chevalier* – and the bird's plumage becomes a knightly plume or *panache*. This is the buckling of elements into a single image, but the fluidity of flight at the same time forbids that kind of solidity. Only with a simultaneous dissolution of the unity can (as with the falling of coals) fire flash. There is a crumpling and bending of the plumage (*buckle* primarily means to bend) and this makes the beauty of the bird so intense that Hopkins has to call on a term of numerical magnitude – *billion* – to justify it. (In an earlier version of the poem the term was *million*, but this is contained in *vermilion* and hence is no true rhyme for it.) *Buckle* refers not only to the kestrel but also to Hopkins's own hidden heart, which collapses in a sense of its unworthiness. But a recovery is made with the revelation of the last lines: he can attain the high-flying loveliness of the Christ-kestrel through service, and buckling and falling and galling – Christ's body was galled – lead to the pride and plume of lowly action.

That the meaning of the poem is not at once apparent, as in, say, Wordsworth's sonnet on Westminster Bridge, and that the meaning once found is complex, bear out the musical analogy I insist on. For what we primarily take in is a structure of sound, which we find to be intelligible enough without rational analysis. But the meaning does not yield itself until we fully understand the distribution of stress and pause, and the variations in tempo enforced by the syllabic patterning. Ultimately the poem cannot be appreciated at all without a skilled performance – which we are yet to have – or a mode of notation which, as with a musical score, indicates precisely what sonic patterns we are meant to hear. The poem is not exactly dead on the page, but it is not completely alive until it soars away from it.

In a later poem – *Spelt from Sibyl's Leaves* – Hopkins uses the musical resources of his prosodic system in both a more complex and a simpler fashion. This is a sonnet, but the lines are octometric or eight-beat with a marked caesura: we are closer to the fourfold beat of common time, with no trouble over that damnable fifth foot of a pentameter. I will not set out the poem, since I do not wish to analyse it, but I will point out some of its very Hopkinsian features. The first line runs thus:

Earnest, earthless, equal, attuneable,|vaulty, voluminous, . . .
stupendous

The seventh foot is silent. Hopkins has borrowed from music the structural rest, which, being locked into the explicit and notated musical pattern, is very different from an imposed rhetorical pause. The device here is not quite legitimate. Any feature of a piece of music has to be balanced by repetition, and properly Hopkins should repeat that pause in some other line – either the last of the octave or the whole poem. As it stands it is mere rhetoric, an element of 'expression' which music would prefer to be notated as a comma or 'tramlines' with a fermata mark above. I have only one other objection before giving unstinted praise to the poem. The final line is this:

Where, selfwrung, selfstrung, sheathe- and shelterless|thoughts agáinst
   thóughts ín groans grind.

The stress marks are Hopkins's own, and I cannot accept the third of them. That *groans* needs full value. Hopkins may have felt that, by displacing the stress, he was modifying a discord that sounded melodramatic to his ear, a flesh-creeping image not in conformity with the high seriousness of the poem. But the prosody of speech demands that *groans* and *grinds* rub against each other and set the teeth on edge.

Hopkins seems to be presenting the following constatation. Evening is coming on, and the dying light is obscuring the essence of the visual world. The 'dapple' or variety of nature, in which the *haecceitas* or 'thisness' of God's creation bids us rejoice and love the Creator, is soon to be hidden in the dark. In history itself, as seen prophetically from Dublin in the winter of 1884–5, a great darkness is approaching, and this will be characterized by a rejection of life's variousness and an insistence on mere abstract opposition, as in Marxist politics. In his last line the poet very vividly suggests the nightmare world which man, forgetting God and God's creation, is proposing to fashion for himself. The urgency and intensity of Hopkins's prophecy (a prophecy all too thoroughly fulfilled) is expressed in a verbal technique which strives for, but cannot quite achieve, the simultaneity of harmony or counterpoint. The English language is not yet, except in the nonsense of 'Jabberwocky', ready for the fusing of two or more words into a new complex entity. Hopkins puns seriously with 'Disremembering, dismembering', where the act of forgetting as expressed in Anglo-Irish is also an act of dissolution, with 'skeined stained veined variety', where rhyme tries to proclaim a near-identity of separate attributes, and with 'earliest stars, earlstars', where a stellar hierarchy is matched by an order of appearance in the sky. There is a brilliant compression in 'part, pen, pack', where three words drawn into a unity by head-rhyme and a common consonant–vowel–consonant structure and yet differentiated sharply in meaning (the ablaut emphasizes this) sum up Christ's prophecy of the Last Judgement. Part the sheep from the goats, pen the sheep in their fold, send the goats packing.

In another sonnet with a more explicit political content – *Tom's Garland: Upon the Unemployed* – the complexity baffles us as it baffled Robert Bridges and Canon Dixon. Here the urge to jam words together into dissonant entities produces *fallowbootfellow* to describe a navvy's workmate: Tom and Dick share the same trench or furrow of untillable earth, yellowish-brown in colour, the colour that gets on to the navvy's boot. Tom 'treads through, prickproof, thick/Thousands of thorns, thoughts'; the thorns and thoughts are the same and require *Finnegans Wake* to render them as *thornts*. Impatience with purely structural words reaches its limit:

> Undenizened, beyond bound
> Of earth's glory, earth's ease, all; no one, nowhere,
> In wide the world's weal; rare gold, bold steel, bare
> In both; care, but share care –
> This, by Despair, bred Hangdog dull; by Rage,
> Manwolf, worse; and their packs infest the age.

No obscurity at the end: Fr Hopkins is finishing a sermon. But the poem as a whole is most unsermonical, a verbal structure rather, which asks for the same response as a piece of complex counterpoint.

Hopkins, in the early days of his novitiate, had been troubled by a conflict between a nature that rejoiced in the sensuous variety or pied beauty of the world and the ascetic discipline of a religious order, but the medieval schoolman Duns Scotus taught him that the *haecceitas* of the created universe, the individual inscapes (Hopkins's word) of all beings were to be rejoiced in as coming from God and leading the rejoicing soul towards God. Hopkins paid a tribute to Duns Scotus, who was believed to have taught at Oxford, and at the same time foresaw the ruin of a gracious town:

Towery city and branchy between towers;
Cuckoo-echoing, bell-swarmèd, lark-charmèd, rook-racked, river-
    rounded;
The dapple-eared lily below thee; that country and town did
Once encounter in, here coped and poisèd powers;

Thou hast a base and brickish skirt there, sours
That neighbour-nature thy grey beauty is grounded
Best in; graceless growth, thou hast confounded
Rural rural keeping – folk, flocks and flowers.

Yet ah! this air I gather and I release
He lived on; these weeds and waters, these walls are what
He haunted who of all men most sways my spirits to peace.

Of realty the rarest-veined unraveller; a not
Rivalled insight, be rival Italy or Greece;
Who fired France for Mary without spot.

This poem, greatly admired, and partially turned into a song of alumnal praise by Dorothy L. Sayers in her *Gaudy Night*, has always worried me somewhat. I cannot altogether blame Hopkins for *Greece*, so easily punned into *grease*, and *spot*, but I feel the lack of a sense of unity of conception – for what has Oxford's decay to do with Duns Scotus, and how does the doctrine of the immaculate conception fit into a structure which has crammed our eyes with the physical and particular, tagged lamely on to the end as it is? It is the second line that particularly disturbs me. It is legitimate sprung rhythm and it stands out as a tour de force, but it calls attention to itself in exactly the manner of a musical phrase. There is nothing wrong with that so long as it is balanced by repetition at a later point in the structure, but there is no repetition and hence no balanced pattern, and hence no legitimacy in its use. It is as if Mozart introduced a melody of ravishing beauty in an exposition but failed to make it reappear in the recapitulation. And, even as a verse statement, it does not quite obey the prosodic rules, since the second half of *river-rounded* has a secondary stress, the primary stress being reserved to *river* of necessity, and *town did, grounded* and *confounded*, all having single stress, which has the force of primary stress, cannot truly rhyme with it.

The third line of the sestet is one of those alleged five-foot lines which the reader tries hard to avoid scanning as a six-beat line. It will only scan in conformity with the rest of the sonnet if we stress *haunt, all, sways, spirits, peace,* and this treats *men* as a disregardable slack to be thrown away. I do not think that Hopkins, introducing the line into conversation, would have spoken it as he enjoins us to speak it here. The whole sonnet is a curious confection where Hopkins is trying things out, playing a surrogate music, his intention less serious than he thinks, triumphant with *folk, flocks and flowers*, a splendid unity, but self-indulgent with *Rural rural* and very nearly silly with *These weeds and waters, these walls are what.*

We have to read such a sonnet, and not the incredible *Deutschland*, to permit doubts about the validity of sprung rhythm and the innovations, or restorations of ancient practice, that go with it. The use of sprung rhythm in the five-beat line, unless it is musically justified by genuine patterning – repetition, variation, calling attention to structure and not to the meaning the structure contains – leads inevitably to prose. Hopkins must have been aware of this, and the use of internal rhyme, head- and end-, vocalic chiming, puns and ablaut, seems to serve the end of insisting that, for all our and his fears to the contrary, the verse is holding. More than anything, his devotion to the sonnet form, which is verse *in excelsis*, seems a means, sometimes a desperate one, of preventing the freedom of the flow from deliquescing into the shapelessness of prose.

It is to be expected that sprung rhythm will work best where it always worked best, long before Hopkins came along – in the four-foot line or its variant the three-foot line, which does not suggest the three-four rhythm of the waltz so much as the one-two-THREE (silent four) of a drummer keeping the pace of the march. Hopkins claimed the invention of sprung rhythm, the system codified, but not of sprung rhythms, which appear regularly in folk rhymes:

> One, two,
> Buckle my shoe . . .
> Thirteen, fourteen,
> Maids are courting.
>
> Misty-moisty was the morn,
> Chilly was the weather.
> There I met an old man
> Dressed all in leather,
> Dressed all in leather
> Against the mist and rain
> It was how-do-you-do and how-do-you-do
> And how-do-you-do again.

In the fragment of a poem on the woodlark Hopkins does no more than follow the example of the folk, with inevitable sophistications of his own:

> The blue wheat-acre is underneath
> And the corn is corded and shoulders its sheaf,
> The ear in milk, lush the sash,
> And crush-silk poppies aflash,
> The blood-gush blade-gash
> Flame-rash rudred
> Bud shelling or broad-shed
> Tatter-tangled and dingle-a-danglèd
> Dandy-hung dainty head.

That he was a superb poet, perhaps the greatest and certainly the most original of the nineteenth century I have no doubt, but it was perhaps always foolish to hail him as a liberator, one who showed the young – when at last, nearly thirty years after his death, they were kindly permitted to read him – how to free themselves from the shackles of a narrow prosodic tradition. Auden and Day Lewis imitated him during their Marxist phase, and, so powerful is Hopkins's personality, their verse seems to present less the coming revolution than the cavortings of an unfrocked and drunken priest. Hopkins's innovations served only his own artistic purpose. It was a complex purpose, and it entailed turning the poetic foot into a musical measure. But it was his own purpose and there could be no progeny. In this respect, apart from others, Hopkins was close to James Joyce.

The difficulty in reading Hopkins remains, and it has much

to do with the lack of a suitable notation. As a diffident coda I append the following quasi-musical transcription of the sestet of *The Windhover*. It will not please literary academics, but musicians will understand.

Brute beauty and valour and act, oh, air, pride, plume, here

Buckle! AND the fire that breaks from thee   then a billion

Times told lovelier, more dangerous, O my chevalier!

No wonder of it: sheer plod makes plough down   sillion

Shine, and blue-bleak embers, ah my dear,

Fall, gall themselves, and gash gold-vermilion.

8
Re Joyce

That James Joyce and Gerard Manley Hopkins resemble each other in their approach to language has often been remarked on, and some not knowledgeable in matters of biography have even spoken of influence. Biographical affinities tease, but they confirm paths parallel and independent. Hopkins was an English convert to Catholicism and a Jesuit priest. Joyce was a cradle Catholic and educated by the Jesuits. Hopkins spent his later days at the University College of Dublin (a Catholic institution intended as an incarnation of Cardinal Newman's *Idea of a University*), where he taught Greek. Joyce graduated at University College but took no Greek. Hopkins followed Duns Scotus and devised a philosophy of inscape and instress. Joyce followed Thomas Aquinas and spoke about epiphanies. Hopkins died in 1889. Joyce was born in 1882. Hopkins's poems were not published until 1918, when Joyce was at work on *Ulysses* and had achieved his own style. Joyce said later in life that he had read Hopkins and considered him a kind of English Mallarmé. How far a common Catholicism, acquired by the one, abandoned by the other, brought them to a common view of art it would be unprofitable to consider here. Not so unprofitable to consider is the truth that both were musicians. Joyce could read music and play the pianoforte, and he had a phenomenally beautiful tenor voice. About Hopkins we already know.

Joyce's musicianship disqualified him as a poet but qualified him as a lyrist. The poems of *Chamber Music* have to be lifted from the page and locked into musical patterns. To have to accept Stephen Dedalus as a fabulous artificer is a fiction that precedes the fiction which contains him. The Stephen of *A*

Portrait of the Artist as a Young Man writes an atrocious villanelle ('Are you not weary of ardent ways?') but he is young and will write better. The Stephen of *Ulysses* will some day write *Ulysses*. The alternative to writing it is being a new Tommy Moore, though one who accepts his presidency over a public urinal ('The meeting of the waters', monologuizes Bloom). In *Ulysses* Joyce fulfils boldly what he has promised in the first story of *Dubliners* – a determination to be fascinated by the sound of words:

Every night as I gazed up at the window I said softly to myself the word paralysis. It had always sounded strangely in my ears, like the word gnomon in the Euclid and the word simony in the Catechism. But now it sounded to me like the name of some maleficent and sinful being. It filled me with fear, and yet I longed to be nearer to it and so look upon its deadly work.

Not only words but phrases, whole sentences. The sound is always important:

By Brady's cottages a boy for the skins lolled, his bucket of offal linked, smoking a chewed fagbutt.

He came nearer and heard a crunching of gilded oats, the gently champing teeth.

A wise tabby, a blinking sphinx, watched from her warm sill.

The bungholes sprang open and a huge dull flood leaked out, flowing together, winding through mudflats all over the level land, a lazy pooling swirl of liquor bearing along wideleaved flowers of its froth.

He foresaw his pale body reclined in it at full, naked, in a womb of warmth, oiled by scented melting soap, softly laved.

To analyse these sentences is to be aware of a kind of oral athleticism, or else of hands playing the keyboard of the phonemic inventory. Joyce composes verbal melodies which seem to subsist independently of the things described. As in true melody, he exploits the possibilities of range – down from *foresaw* up to *pale*, down to *body*, forward to *reclined*, up and back to *full*, forward to *naked*, back and up to *womb*, down to *warmth*, gliding from down to up in the diphthong *oiled*, and then it is time for repetition of the front close *e* of *scented*, *melting*; at the same time there is a less obtrusive melody played on the consonants and semivowels – *womb of warmth, scented, soap, softly*.

This sounds fanciful and metaphorical – like Eliot describing Edmund Spenser as the great master of melody – and must always be so until we are clear about the relationship between the acoustics of speech and the acoustics of music. Helmholtz, as I remember but cannot now confirm, explained the vowels as the product of two fixed pitches, absolute pitch operating in vocalic production though not necessarily in the sphere of tonality. It is enough for me to rely on my ear and accept only an analogy between the chromatic scale and the double ladder of the vowels and diphthongs, as enshrined in the mnemonics 'Who would know aught of art must learn, act, and then take his ease' and 'Fear the poor outside the door; beware of power, avoid desire'. In preparing a Schönbergian *Grundstimmung* you must arrange the twelve notes of the chromatic scale in a significant order (whatever *significant* can be made to mean) without the repetition of a note which would seem, undemocratically, to make it more important than the others. To create a Joyce melody you have more choice of sounds, but a similar system of selection is involved. And, I say again, the melody often seems independent of referent, an aspect of the technique of Flaubertian objectivity, the artist removed from his handiwork. Identify the phonemes in the following. You will find the double inventory at work, as well as a cunning, and essentially musical, exploitation of vocalic contrast:

She dances in a foul gloom where gum burns with garlic. A sailorman, rustbearded, sips from a beaker rum and eyes her. A long and seafed silent rut. She dances, capers, wagging her sowish haunches and her hips, on her gross belly flapping a ruby egg.

It is characteristic of the Joyce sentence in *Ulysses* that it should draw attention to itself as a sonic entity, though the greatness of his cunning ensures that it also fits its referent. The following could not be simpler.

The vesta in the clergyman's uplifted hand consumed itself in a long soft flame and was let fall. At their feet its red speck died: and mouldy air closed round them.

But to explain why *fore* and *frankly* are correct in the following requires several lines of commentary:

Two carfuls of tourists passed slowly, their women sitting fore, gripping frankly the handrests.

The words surprise as a true melody surprises. *Frankly* is normally used to modify statements in which a social judgement is made, but here it seems to mean 'in awareness that there was no real need to grip the handrests, since a jolting passage was not to be expected, and in a spirit of mild defiance of the judgement of onlookers who might doubt the necessity of such a measure of safety'. *Fore* is there not because there is any nautical connotation in the passage (though it comes in the chapter which parallels the passage of the Argonauts among the wandering rocks) but because it is shorter than *in the front.* If there is surprise, it is not wanton and gratuitous, any more than in Hopkins. Joyce joins Hopkins in hating 'aquacities of language' and always avoids the emptily structural when he can. He prefers the compound adjective to the adjectival phrase or clause. *Let fall* is better than *permitted to fall.* Rewrite that passage about the sailor and the dancer in orthodox prose and you lose the feeling as well as the music:

She is dancing in a foul-smelling gloomy place where lamps burn and give off an odour of gum and garlic. A sailorman with a beard the colour of rust sips rum from a beaker and watches her. In his eyes glows a lust which a long sea voyage of enforced celibacy has nourished. As she dances and capers around, wagging her haunches, fat as a sow's, and wriggling her hips, he sees flapping on her gross belly a cheap jewel big as an egg and of a ruby colour.

In the 'Wandering Rocks' episode of *Ulysses* Joyce temporarily gets outside the Homeric myth which sustains the seventeen other chapters and borrows the myth of Jason and the Argonauts and their careful navigation between the clashing Symplegades. He wishes to show Dublin and certain of its citizens walking their city from an aspect not temporal but spatial. He constructed the chapter with a map and a stopwatch in front of him and sought, impossible task, to present a counterpoint of action. He has eighteen brief sections, corresponding to the eighteen long episodes of the entire book, and each of these contains the solidity, or wandering rock, of a peripatetic citizen or group of citizens. These both clash and do not clash with each other. In the action they keep their distance but in the technique of description they butt in where they are not expected.

– Where would I get money? Mr Dedalus asked. There is no one in Dublin would lend me fourpence.
– You got some, Dilly said, looking in his eyes.
– How do you know that? Mr Dedalus asked, his tongue in his cheek.
Mr Kernan, pleased with the order he had booked, walked boldly along James's street.
– I know you did, Dilly answered. Were you in the Scotch house now?

Mr Dedalus and his daughter are standing outside Dillon's auction rooms. Mr Kernan is some distance away, but he intrudes for a sentence to remind us of the simultaneity of two actions. Temple Bar is a long way from Phoenix Park, which the viceroy and his court are just leaving:

While he waited in Temple bar McCoy dodged a banana peel with gentle pushes of his toe from the path to the gutter. Fellow might damn easy get a nasty fall there coming along tight in the dark.
The gates of the drive opened wide to give egress to the viceregal cavalcade.
– Even money, Lenehan said returning. I knocked against Bantam Lyons in there going to back a bloody horse someone gave him that hasn't an earthly.

Joyce clicks his stopwatch and notes another simultaneity.
The science which presides over this chapter is engineering. There are several references to one particular piece of engineering – the clock or watch, which is an organization of parts which function together but do not get entangled with each other. The city is such a machine: Joyce wants to give us a model of a labyrinthine organism which can be viewed as a mechanism: his concern is synchronic, not diachronic, but the very nature of literature, which functions only in time (and time is not the same thing as the timepiece which measures it) forbids a true counterpoint of action. Music, unlike literature, can be both synchronic and diachronic: we can read or hear it horizontally, from left to right, and vertically, from top to bottom. This is an endowment which Joyce envies. He can match it only through trickery. But, once started on the mechanical polyphony of the

'Wandering Rocks' episode, he is committed to the composition of a human polyphony. The chapter that follows finds its Homeric counterpart in the story of Odysseus and the Sirens, the presiding organ is the ear, and the presiding art is music. He proposes to write a fugue of more than Bachian size and complexity. At the same time, of course, he knows it cannot be done with mere monodic words.

The chapter begins with a catalogue of disjunct phrases and vocables, ending like this:

Last rose Castille of summer left bloom I feel so sad alone.
Pwee! Little wind piped wee.
True men. Lid Ker Cow De and Doll. Ay, ay. Like you men. Will lift your tschink with tschunk.
Fff! Oo!
Where bronzes from anear? Where gold from afar? Where hoofs?
Rrrpr. Kraa. Kraandl.
Then, not till then. My eppripfftaph. Be pfrwritt.
Done.
Begin!

Joyce is never averse to mystification, so long as it can be cleared up sooner or later in good orthodox Thomistic Aristotelian style. This passage very much interested the Allied censors of the First World War, who suspected that it might be a message for the enemy in code. But all Joyce's codes are easily broken and they stand outside the trivial concerns of nations. What he is doing here is laying out for our inspection the bones that litter the isle of the Sirens. He is also giving us the themes out of which his musical fabric will be woven. The final word is an injunction to the orchestra to begin playing it, and it evokes Walther's first trial song in *Die Meistersinger*.

Joyce's Sirens are no man-eaters. They are the two barmaids of the Ormond Hotel, 'cowering under their reef of counter', drinking tea not blood. Leopold Bloom comes to the restaurant of the hotel to eat dinner and to write a letter covertly to his penfriend Martha Clifford. He will eat liver and bacon (which, if we wish, play the tune EADBAC) and drink cider (CDE). The cider will combine with the burgundy he has taken at lunchtime to promote flatulence: he will be ready at the end of the fugue to play a coda from his coda or tail. The chapter is crammed

with music, specifically Joyce's own art of song, coming from
the music room where the piano has just been tuned. But where
is the fugue? The Sirens themselves represent the subject, and
Bloom is the answer (the subject restated in another voice, a fifth
higher or fourth lower). The countersubject, or contrapuntal
accompaniment to the answer and then to each restatement of
the subject, is represented by Blazes Boylan, who comes to the
Ormond bar – or counter, since he is the countersubject – for a
drink before going off to fornicate with Bloom's wife Molly.
Joyce dares not press the formal parallel too hard. The Sirens do
not possess musical connotations less fanciful than their names
– Mina Kennedy and Lydia Douce (Minor Ke. . . .y and Lydian
mode; Milton asks to be wrapped in soft, or douce, Lydian airs).
When Joyce first presents them, Bloom is on his way to the hotel
by foot and Boylan in a horse-cab. They can be symbolized in
visual or sonic shorthand. Misses Kennedy and Douce have
respectively bronze-coloured and blond hair – 'bronze by gold';
Bloom is associated with the song 'The Bloom is on the Rye';
Boylan by 'jingle jaunty jingle', which stands not only for his cab
but, proleptically, for the bedsprings in Bloom's house. 'Horn',
an appropriate term in a musical context, stands both for Boylan's impatient lust and Bloom's cuckolding.

Between the fugal statements there have to be episodes, and
these are provided by Simon Dedalus, tenor, and Ben Dollard,
bass. Mr Dedalus appropriately sings the aria '*M'appari*' from
the opera *Martha* while Bloom is writing to its eponym's name-
sake. When music sounds Joyce's prose responds:

A duodene of birdnotes chirruped bright treble answer under sensitive
hands. Brightly the keys, all twinkling, linked, all harpsichording,
called to a voice to sing the strain of dewy morn, of youth, of love's
leavetaking, life's, love's morn.

We hear a tremolo: 'Her wavyavyeavyheavyeavyeevyey hair un-
comb:'d.' Chords are played staccato: 'I. Want. You.' There are
hollow fifths: 'Blmstdp', the vowels of 'Bloom stood up' omitted
on the analogy of suppressed thirds in common chords. One
vulgar trick – one of the Sirens lifting her skirt and snapping her
garter for Boylan's delectation – is there because it is known as
Sonnez la cloche. It is punningly answered by the bell of the

sandwich stand. When Boylan leaves to keep his assignment with Molly Bloom, the prose prepares to forsake reasonable syntax and mirror only his animal excitement:

Atrot in heat, heatseated. *Cloche. Sonnez la. Cloche. Sonnez la.* Slower the mare went up the hill by the Rotunda, Rutland Square. Too slow for Boylan, blazes Boylan, impatience Boylan, joggled the mare . . . Jog jig jogged stopped. Dandy tan shoe of dandy Boylan socks skyblue clocks came light to earth.

Boylan has arrived at No. 7 Eccles Street, where Molly Bloom awaits him. She likes the novels of Paul de Kock. Obligingly Joyce elevates Boylan into that pornographic master:

One rapped on a door, one tapped with a knock, did he knock Paul de Kock, with a loud proud knocker, with a cock carracarracarra cock. Cockcock.

The noble structure of a fugue is, finally, mocked, as is the whole heavenly art of music. Prose can only get near to music if, shedding meaning, it approaches noise. We have reached the final stretto, which requires a pedal-point. The blind piano tuner has left his tuning fork at the Ormond and is coming back for it. His stick goes 'Tap. Tap. Tap' and, though it is to be associated with the absolute pitch of his tuning instrument, it is only a noise sounding under other noises – Bloom's borborygms, the clink of glasses – 'Tschink. Tschunk' – the clanking of a tram – 'Kran, kran, kran' – and the noises of Boylan's lust. Only the final words of the patriot Robert Emmet, which Bloom reads in a shop window, make sense, but they are drowned by his own visceral gurglings, the row of the street, and the jingling of the bedsprings. They are also to be debased in the chapter which comes immediately after, where the chauvinistic 'citizen' makes nonsense of patriotism.

Joyce is being cruel in his implication that even the noblest of music primarily serves the senses. It pretends to be about love but really evokes the rhythms of lust. Separate it from sense, meaning words as semantic units, and it is not distinguishable from noise (John Cage would agree). It is because literature has no power to imitate the sound of music that it is led to mockery of its sister art. Structure, however, is a different matter, but Joyce knew all along that he could not reproduce the form of a fugue. Musical structure and literary structure meet in *Ulysses* where they are unannounced in the symbolism, in the episodes where medicine and magic respectively preside.

The 'Oxen of the Sun' chapter is set in the Holles Street maternity hospital, which is in the charge of a certain A. Horne. The name is historically verifiable but is most convenient for Joyce's symbolism, since it evokes oxen, emblems of fertility, in the duplicated form 'horhorn' of the opening invocation to both the sun, father of fecundity and divine owner of the oxen, and the moon, whose goddess Hecate is the matron of midwives. But 'horhorn' has also been one of the noises associated with Blazes Boylan as lecher and Bloom as cuckold. We are being warned to expect reminiscence from earlier sections of the novel, and the reminiscence is, as it turns out, in the service of form not meaning.

Joyce wishes to make his prose imitate the process of gestation, and so he presents the fusion of Anglo-Saxon and Latin, representing the male and female principles, and the subsequent development of the English language in the womb of the past to burst out at last as the tongue of the future. He gives us a history of English prose style, which is a fair analogue of the growth of the foetus, and he naturally has to concentrate on form more than content. In the preceding chapters he has given us content enough, and perhaps the reader will not be able to take much more without a sense of surfeit. The time has come to fantasize this content, digest it, make it serve prose structures without separable meaning – in a word, musicalize it. Here Joyce is imitating the style of Thomas de Quincey:

Onward to the dead sea they tramp to drink, unslaked and with horrible gulpings, the salt somnolent inexhaustible flood. And the equine portent grows again, magnified in the deserted heavens, nay to heaven's own magnitude, till it looms, vast, over the house of Virgo. And lo, wonder of metempsychosis, it is she, the everlasting bride, harbinger of the daystar, the bride, ever virgin. It is she, Martha, thou lost one, Millicent, the young, the dear, the radiant. How serene does she now arise, a queen among the Pleiades, in the penultimate antelucan hours, shod in sandals of bright gold, coifed with a veil of what do you call it gossamer! It floats, it flows about her starborn flesh and loose it streams emerald, sapphire, mauve and heliotrope, sustained on currents of cold interstellar wind, winding, coiling, simply swirling writhing in the skies a mysterious writing till after a myriad metamorphoses of symbol, it blazes, Alpha, a ruby and triangled sign upon the forehead of Taurus.

This does not mean very much. It cannot be paraphrased. And even the meaning of its component words is lacking if we have not paid close attention to the preceding chapters of the book. Early in the morning Bloom meditated on the Dead Sea and the diaspora of the Jews. The 'equine portent' is the winner of the Ascot Gold Cup, Throwaway, which Bloom tipped unconsciously by saying he was going to throw his newspaper away. The references to virgins combine Martha Clifford, to whom Bloom has written, his daughter Milly, and a girl encountered on Sandymount strand, Gerty MacDowell. The word 'metempsychosis' was puzzled over early in the day by Molly Bloom, who folk-etymologized it to 'met him pike hoses'. Mr Dedalus has sung in the Ormond music room the aria '*M'appari*' from *Martha*, with its line 'Come thou lost one, come thou dear one'. The morning light appeared to Bloom as a girl in gold sandals; he devised, off to ease his bowels, a series of costumes for Ponchielli's 'Dance of the Hours'. Alpha in the Greek alphabet is a stylization of the head of an ox; it is confused with the delta which is the shape of the island of the Oxen of the Sun. A red triangle is the trade mark on the bottles of Bass in the medical students' commonroom where the action of the chapter takes place.

With this fantasy, and others like it, Joyce prepares us for the much more ambitious reprises of the 'Circe' episode, which may be taken as the exhaustive development section of the *Ulysses* symphony. Anything that has appeared earlier has now to appear again. In the first chapter Buck Mulligan, taking off his dressing gown and saying, 'Mulligan is stripped of his garments', adds: 'And going forth he met Butterly.' This is a ridiculous deformation of 'And going forth he wept bitterly', but the name Butterly, having been pronounced, has to make formal sense sooner or later. Butterly appears briefly and otherwise inexplicably in the 'Circe' episode, a farmer with a turnip. Old images are fused into new ones. Stephen's mother arises from the dead, and Buck Mulligan, seated on top of the Martello tower at

Sandycove, dressed in jester's motley, weeps tears of molten butter into an open scone. This combines the lodging which Stephen and Mulligan have shared, the cruel clowning of Mulligan, and the tea he took with the Englishman Haines at the DBC tea rooms.

The setting of the 'Circe' episode is the brothel district of Dublin, where men are turned into swine and, indeed, into a whole menagerie of slobbering beasts, and language has to be reduced to gibberish. But the gibberish is carefully contrived out of the materials already presented. The fracturing of speech is more musical than mimetic. The principle of thematic balance is totally fulfilled. In a symphonic movement no theme may appear unless it is to be transformed in the free fantasia or development section, or, more simply, granted a reappearance. This is the 'Circe' technique. In the 'dance of death' which takes place before the ghastly resurrection of Stephen's mother, the following represents its rhythm:

Bang fresh barang bang of lacquey's bell, horse, nag, steer, piglings, Conmee on Christass lame crutch and leg sailor in cockboat armfolded ropepulling bitching stamp hornpipe through and through, Baraabum! On nags, hogs, bellhorses, Gadarene swine, Corny in coffin. Steel shark stone onehandled Nelson, two trickies Frauenzimmer plumstained from pram falling bawling. Gum, he's a champion. Fuseblue peer from barrel rev. evensong Love on hackney jaunt Blazes blind coddoubled bicyclers Dilly with snowcake no fancy clothes. Then in last wiswitchback lumbering up and down bump mashtub sort of viceroy and reine relish for tublumber bumpshire rose. Baraabum!

There is not one element there, however nonsensical-seeming, that does not find its provenance in the previous parts of the book. But the combination is a free one and is more concerned with sound than meaning. Yet Joyce's intention is formal as well as narrative: the musician in him cannot permit any element to justify its presence solely in terms of fictional realism. In the first chapter of the book, Buck Mulligan performs a kind of black mass, pretending to turn his shaving water into blood. In the last chapter Molly menstruates. Mock blood is balanced by real blood. The first word of the book is *Stately*; the last is *yes:* *s . . . y* balances *y . . . s*. This is essentially musical, and to the fiction reader who demands no more than character and action it will seem certainly supererogatory and probably mad.

The free fantasia of 'Circe' presents the human mind set upon by bad magic which kills the rational and promotes the bestial. Reason returns and the spell is exorcised. In *Finnegans Wake* there appears to be a flight from reason which the author has no intention of reversing. Yet the irrationality is rationally based. Joyce is presenting his story in the form of a dream, and reason tells him that waking language, with its emphasis on discrete entities and restricted movement through time, will not serve his end. He has to contrive an oneiric language. One of the meanings of the Anglo-Saxon word *dream* was music. It is not surprising that here, freed from the limitations of daytime lexis and syntax, language should at last consistently start to behave like music.

Finnegans Wake presents, like the poems of Hopkins, a reading problem. It has to be read aloud; it has to be performed professionally. But it cannot be wholly freed from the page. We need the score, as we need the score of a work of the Viennese atonal school, to perceive patterns clearer to the eye than to the ear. The name of Joyce's sleeping hero is Mr Porter – appropriate for a man who keeps a pub in Chapelizod, carries Guinness up from the cellar, and bears the load of a sexual sin on his back – but in his dream his name changes to Humphrey Chimpden Earwicker. The initials are more important than the full name. They can be newly filled out to such significant tropes as 'Here Comes Everybody' (Earwicker is ourselves) and our 'Human Conger Eel' (he is slippery, he is an animated phallus), but they are also sewn into the fabric of the text like a monogram. When we meet them in 'Howth Castle and Environs' (he is not only all men, but all cities, and one city in particular) or in 'hecitency' (a rearrangement of the letters which does not harm the recognizability: we are being reminded of the Piggot forgeries which incriminated Parnell – one of HCE's avatars – and mispelt *hesitancy*), we know that the hero is around. HCE is, incidentally, a musical phrase if we follow German nomenclature and take H as B natural, but Joyce does not exploit the name musically. Still, we cannot help remembering that *Tristan und Isolde* ends in the key of H, and that HCE is sometimes the comic King Mark the gulls quark at.

It is not my aim here to analyse the work in terms of its content; I wish merely to show how dream, permitting the fusion of real-life referents in free fantasias, is naturally conveyed in a verbal technique which turns words into chords and discourse into counterpoint. One of Joyce's simpler dream-puns is 'cropse', which combines two opposed images – corpse and crops. We have to see it as well as hear it. We recognize the justness of the fusion, a circular process – dead flesh nourishing the earth to produce living flesh which will in its turn become dead flesh – being presented as an instantaneous figure. This is Joyce's method. It is usually more complex.

Earwicker is accused of a sexual crime in the Phoenix Park and is hailed like this: 'O foenix culprit!' Clear enough on the surface, but under the surface is St Augustine's *O felix culpa* – O happy sin in the Garden of Eden, since it brought God to earth as our redeemer. The nickname given to O'Mara, 'an exprivate secretary of no fixed abode', is 'Mildew Lisa'. He is one of those responsible for spreading foul rumours about HCE and the term is comically opprobrious, but it echoes '*Mild und leise*', the opening words of Isolde's scene in Wagner's music drama. Tristran and Earwicker alike have been guilty of illicit love, but Earwicker is also King Mark II, or Mark Twain. Shaun, one of HCE's twin sons, a kind of singing demagogue, is described as 'mielodorous' – meaning that he is melodious, malodorous, but also smells of honey. In the prophetic phrase 'the abnihilization of the etym' the atom is not merely split but, as atomic truth or meaning, it is restored out of nothing. All these chords combine opposed ideas, but the conjunction is never a mere occasional shock: the action of the book takes place in the mythical year 1132, which yokes falling (32 feet per second per second) and resurrection (if we count 11 on our fingers we have to go back to the beginning again) and finds its geometrical figure in the circle. If death and resurrection are aspects of each other ('cropse'), then the whole lexis is necessarily based on the seventh type of ambiguity.

If we look further than isolated word-chords and examine whole paragraphs, we shall see multiple counterpoint in action:

When old the wormd was a gadden and Anthea first unfoiled her limbs

wanderloot was the way the wood wagged where opter and apter were
samuraised twimbs. They had their mutthering ivies and their mur-
dhering idies and their mouldhering iries in that muskat grove but
there'll be bright plinnyflowers in Calomella's cool bowers when the
magpyre's babble towers scorching and screeching from the
ravenindove.

In the first place it is necessary to read this aloud in order to
recognize that it is a piece of rhymed verse, not prose. In the
second we have to know that there is a waking datum underneath
it – Joyce's favourite passage from Quinet, which describes the
eternal recurrence of flowers laughing from the ruined towers of
wars and sieges, as fresh today as in the days of Pliny. The
flower theme takes us to the primal garden, which has a worm
or dragon in it. The three children of HCE are there, the girl
Isobel (Iseult la belle or the Isolde who sings *'Mild und leise'*) as
Anthea or the first flower, the boys, twin limbs of their father,
as 'samuraised twimbs', and all support a conspiracy against their
father, representative of the outworn world the children must
take over and renew. The ivy, like a mass of watching eyes, will
see murder on the Ides of March. The rainbow of peace, bloom-
ing as an iris, will lose its colours and decay. The musky grove
is full of guns. HCE, who has defiled the garden of the Phoenix
Park with his sins, must be burnt, so that, rising fresh once more
from the phoenix ashes, peace and fragrance may return to Eden.
But then the whole process must start again, the circle turn for
ever.

The contrapuntal technique is easily learned, and the skill of
the game lies in convincingly blending arbitrary collocations of
ideas. If one is drunk the whole year round, then the names of
the months become Ginyouvery Pubyoumerry Parch Grapeswill
Tray Juinp Droolie Sawdust Siptumbler Actsober Newwinebar
Descendbeer. If Charles Dickens is a cook as well as a novelist
he must produce works like *Charred Limes, Grate Expectorations,
The Cold Curried Sausagy Chop, Our Muttonual Fried, Halibut
Twiced, Pickweak Peppers* and *Snack Elly's Knucklebone.* Shakespeare as a cat wrote *The Tompist* and as a jobbing printer *Pamphlet Prints of Penmark* and as an American *All Swell that End?
Swell.* If the legend of Martin Luther's having six toes on his

left foot has to be retold, and Luther has to be both a musical instrument and a bird, then the following might serve:

To bigsing mitt (and there are some of sinminstral hexachordiality who have cheeped Nine! Nine! to so supernumerapodical a valgar halluxination of their Herro) it was harpbuzzing tags when, achording to Fussboden and Sexfanger, the gamut and spinet of it was (A! O! says Rholy with his Alfa Romega) that funf went into sox and Queen Kway was half dousin to her sixther, so that our truetone orchestinian luter (may his bother martins swallow rondines and roundels of chelidons and their oves be eaved on the belfriars), deptargmined not to be housemartined by his frival sinxters (Ping! wint the strongs of the eadg be guitarnberg), put hexes on his hocks and said sex is funf, which is why he aspierred to a dietty of worms and married anon (Moineau! Consparrocy!) after he had strummed his naughntytoo frets on the door (fish can nosh tenders) and was eggscomeinacrated.

There is no limit to punning if, like Joyce, we draw on foreign languages to eke out English (Joyce's English can be called Eurish). Whether this kind of thing is worth doing is another matter.

Finnegans Wake calls itself a 'crossmess parzle', which combines a Christmas parcel and a crossword puzzle: it is a toy, a box of tricks, a game. It is also a serious attempt to find a verbal symbology for a mental experience that fills up a good third of our lives. If dreams look like games played by the unconscious, nevertheless they are games which nature considers important and they cannot be laughed off. It might have been enough for Joyce to confine himself, as he seemed to be doing in the thirties, when *Anna Livia Plurabelle* and *Here Comes Everybody* appeared as pamphlets, to a briefer demonstration of dream language, or oneiroglot, than a massive book, but it would be churlish to reject the labours of seventeen years, exacerbated as they were by near-blindness. *Finnegans Wake* perhaps had to be written as a horrid warning to musical literary men not to let two irreconcilable arts mate and beget a stillborn hybrid. Certainly, it cannot be repeated, and many will say thank God. But, possessing as we do the glorious triumph of *Ulysses* and the glorious failure of *Finnegans Wake*, we can no longer evade a binary view of the art of the novel. The novel can be a plain representation of human life; it can be a structure which yearns towards the condition of music. Perhaps it is at its greatest when, like *Ulysses*, it is both. But to understand that the major literary form of our age is, of its nature, subject to contrary tugs is the beginning of one kind of aesthetic wisdom.

9

Contrary Tugs

Words, as I have already said, and perhaps too often, cannot subsist without referents. In the beginning was not the word but the thing. Samuel Johnson, in the Preface to his *Dictionary*, said that he was not so far gone in lexicography as to forget that, while words were the daughters of men, things were the sons of heaven. A word differs from a musical note or phrase in being an attempt to find in the movements of the mouth and larynx a means of symbolizing external phenomena – and these external phenomena include highly internal sensations and emotions. There are two things in the world – language and everything that is not language.

Whether language began as an attempt to find iconic equivalents for sense data we shall never know. We have few words like *moon*, which tries to express both the roundness and the height of the heavenly body by making a circle of the lips and by raising the tongue as high as possible. The vast majority of our words are, as Saussure puts it, inert and arbitrary. Inert in that they resist change, arbitrary in that their structure bears no essential relationship to their referents. Once we are committed to the use of language, we have to articulate and phonate inert and arbitrary sounds which, by a consensus of the society to which we belong, signify certain things, feelings and events. And also concepts like God and beauty, abstractions like number, ethical and aesthetic judgements. We all recognize that language is in the service of a prelinguistic reality.

A highly sophisticated society will always be tempted to accord language a reality of its own. Members of the Women's Liberation Movement see in certain words the malevolent magic of male oppression, forgetting the inertness and arbitrariness. Thus, a woman with the name Newman will wish to change it to Newwoman. Chairmen are already called chairpersons. It has been proposed by one American woman that the term testimony, possessing too masculine an etymology, must have a female counterpart in ovarimony. For both the sexes everywhere it has been discovered that syntax makes its own ghostly sense, and that if a statement has a coherent structure, its semantic burden is of no importance. Heads of state, whose trade is evasion, are expert in the manipulation of sentences with little meaning. 'The nuclear capability of the national entity under consideration has not at this time been rendered susceptible of any viable clarification in terms of its belligerent capacity and I hope that answers your question Jim.' The trouble with even sincere and sensible statements is that they can deal only in either tautology or lies. 'Chinese women have exquisite legs.' That cannot be true since there have to be exceptions. 'Some Chinese women have exquisite legs.' That is true but it is not worth saying.

Literary artists, who take words seriously, or consider that they do, despise political gobbledygook. They also avoid tautology by telling lies which are termed figurative statements. April is not really the cruellest month, and when Sweeney says 'Life is death' he is uttering nonsense. But there is a sense in which we can be forced to take a fresh look at reality only by accepting its contradictions. For, as *Finnegans Wake* propounds at great length, life is circular and the beginning of a circle is also its end; life is not a rectilinear continuum. Thus the season of renewal is cruel because renewal entails the death of the old, and we may have committed ourselves to the old. Life is death because it moves towards death from its very beginning. The discourse of ordinary life avoids this kind of truth and hence avoids statements of a poetic nature.

Now the poet's awareness of the circularity of life, in which things can be expressed in terms of their opposites, sometimes leads him to an aesthetic in which anything can be expressed as anything. If life can be death, it can also, and perhaps more reasonably, be a bowl of cherries, an automobile, a force 9 wind, or a black dog. Take it further: life is a unity, and hence all aspects of life are relevant to each other. Draw from the unconscious an arbitrary string of words, and they can all be made to stand in a tenable relation. Perspex, keyboard, cognac, magenta, spider, yoghurt, eyes, forge, epilogue – I have let these drift up from the depths to be set down on paper, and it only remains to arrange them in a pattern. 'The spider forges its perspex keyboard, eyes the yoghurt magenta and its cognac epilogue.' That can easily be dismissed as nonsense, but the cautious will prefer to speak of surrealism. It is not easy to write nonsense, since everything relates to everything else. A runcible spoon and a runcible hat have in common the attribute of runcibility. If they did not possess it they would be unruncible or, more likely, irruncible. If it means nothing else, runcible means belonging to the world of Edward Lear.

The impossibility of nonsense may strike a certain kind of writer with despair. I mean, perhaps, the writer who envies music its self-referring components, who would be a composer if he could because he distrusts words, who distrusts words because he distrusts what words mean (Edward Lear's psychotic condition?). Aware of the unity of the outside world as mirrored in the unity of his own mind, and of the difficulty of making words, aspects of the unity, transcend the unity, he may be driven to destroy syntax. For syntax expresses the relationship between objects, and a 'well-formed' sentence confirms external reality. It is because my sentence about the spider and its perspex keyboard is well formed that it seems to make sense. To make an ill-formed sentence like 'Boy out now Wellington transfuse coop' is to write true nonsense, but we are so structured that we will find meaning in it if we can. We will take it that the printer has erred, and that a boy just out of prison in the town of Wellington is willing to cooperate in giving blood for a transfusion. Or perhaps the writer is reproducing the effect on the reader's eye of the rapid skimming of a page of newsprint (compare the 'fold-in' technique of William Burroughs). But no writer will deliberately choose syntactical nonsense in order to free language (hence himself) from the external world. Such nonsense, he knows, is a symptom of dementia, and art should be the sole sanity in a mad world. Nonsense is cognate with glossolalia, in which phonemes become phones, and that too is a disease.

In writing surrealistic verse to be accompanied by the highly
structured musical rhythms of William Walton, the late Edith
Sitwell played with the principle of discontinuous narrative:

> When Sir Beelzebub
> Called for his syllabub in the hotel in hell,
> Blue as the waves of the sea were the gendarmerie,
> Rocking and shocking the barmaid.
> Nobody comes to give him his rum
> But the rim of the sky hippopotamus-glum
> Enhances the chances to bless with a benison
> Alfred Lord Tennyson crossing the bar laid
> With pale vegetation of pale deputations
> Of temperance workers, all signed In Memoriam,
> Hoping in glory to trip up the Laureate's feet,
> Moving in classical metres.
> Like Balaclava the lava came down from the roof
> And the sea's blue wooden gendarmerie
> Took him in charge while Beelzebub calls for his rum.
> None of them come!

(I quote from the memory of being involved in a performance.)
Things happen here because of free association, helped with
rhymes. Beelzebub has nothing to do with Tennyson (whose
world is so very concisely evoked: Dame Edith's heart was there,
and not in hell), except for the link 'bar' with its two meanings
– a true enharmonic chord. This is acceptable as elegant and
amusing, and the mocking deference to the principle of unity –
Beelzebub, the hotel and the gendarmerie are there at the end
because they are there at the beginning – is the only element we
might demur at.

Clearly, poetry of a surrealistic kind can, as a dream can, free
the imagination from the trammels of daily cause and effect.
Words are not freed from referents, but the referents can become
confused and ambiguous. The multiple referent of a narrative,
to which the atomic referents of the component words defer, can
exhibit discontinuity. This is not the way a novel is written. The
writing of a novel entails an approach to language not far removed
from the world of ordinary discourse. A bar is either what Tennyson crossed or a place which serves rum (probably not sylla-
bubs); one cannot change into the other. The novel form calls

for a rigidity of control of the linguistic medium which forbids the freer art of the poet. Language must be transparent, not opaque. The reader concentrates on character and plot, and he is not greatly concerned with how these properties are conveyed. He would be happy if, by a miracle, the book he is reading could change into a cinema. He makes only one stipulation of the author – that language shall not get in the way.

The novel was, with certain eccentric exceptions, such as *Tristram Shandy*, traditionally a form not attractive to fantasists or poets. From Richardson on it conveyed scenes from a kind of real life in a no-nonsense style. In Fielding it admitted patches of mock-Homeric pastiche, but Fielding usually kept things plain, inviting his readers to follow the exploits of characters so convincingly drawn that they seemed to transcend language. Even Dickens, who is more given to surrealism than many recognize, could create personages who lived as much in their illustrations as in the text. With Joyce's *Ulysses* there was, if not for the first time in the history of the novel at least never before so massively and consistently, a preoccupation with language, symbol and form which seemed to fight against the traditional concerns of the genre. It has frequently been said by critics of *Ulysses* that it is at those points in the novel where the reader has the most right to clarity of narration that Joyce most perversely decides to obfuscate. In the maternity hospital in Holles Street, Bloom and Stephen have their first prolonged encounter, and it is here that Joyce emits the squid-ink of literary pastiche and parody: doubts are cast on the seriousness of his fictional intention. But Joyce's characters are so solid that no amount of formal eccentricity can really obscure them – so solid indeed that it is possible to call on them to engage the obstacles of style in order to defeat them. Even in *Finnegans Wake* the Porter or Earwicker family retains its identity, however much it puts on historical fancy dress and speaks foreign tongues. It is when the novelist is tempted to let language pull away from the referent of situation, or the complex of situations that is the novel itself, that the reader becomes uneasy.

In his juvenile novella *An Island in the Moon*, William Blake makes one of his characters shove his head in the fire and run flaming round the room. Then he denies his fiction, calling it a lie: he was merely playing a joke on the reader. In *Tristram Shandy* Laurence Sterne has Lefevre close his eyes in death, then open them again, then close them, then open them. 'Shall I go on? No.' Both authors know that language is a mode of manipulation; they have the power to use it as they will, though usually the novelist enters into a covenant with the reader to play fair, to grant an autonomy to his characters with which he will not wantonly interfere. Virginia Woolf, belonging to the age of a freer, or more poetic, aesthetic of the novel, can, in *Orlando*, make her protagonist live three centuries and change sex halfway through. In his short story about Averroes, Jorge Luis Borges paints a detailed and convincing picture of the Islamic philosopher spending an evening with his friends and then returning home to resume work on his commentary on Aristotle. In the *Poetics* he meets the word *tragoedia* and does not understand it, but he writes: 'There are many examples of tragedy in the Koran.' At once the scene dissolves; Averroes is revealed as nothing more than a verbal structure which the author who made it has a right to unmake. We have lost confidence in Averroes as a scholar; we had better lose confidence in him as a living entity; we had better annihilate him. This can be done if the author wishes, though normally he does not because of his contract with the reader. The whole aesthetic of Borges is based on the fictionality, or feigning, of his *ficciones*. A fiction is a lie, and a lie ought to be exploded. The referent of a name being only a creation of the author's, the name itself is as close to self-reference as you can get. If, in the Borgesian view, I write 'the one-eyed wart-nosed family butcher', the reader has no true right to set up that character, like a real being, in time and space. He is dependent on the words which describe him, and those words are in my control.

Some years ago I wrote a novel in which one of the characters is an amateur jockey, hence small. Of him I said at one point: 'He got up, or down, from his chair.' This caused great anxiety among readers and those reviewers who noticed the passage. They could have reconciled the opposed images under a different covenant, that of the surrealist poet, but in a novel they expected the language to be a neutral glass through which they could view an ordinary world of unequivocal actions. They wanted my book to behave like a film, and yet not one of those trick films in which a character can be made to get up and down at the same time – an honest to goodness piece of visuality, rather, recording a known universe of cause and effect. The novels which cause least trouble to the reader should, we are tempted to think, have been films in the first place.

The easily filmable novel belongs to a category which I shall call Class 1 fiction. I shall reserve this designation to the fiction of our own time: in the pre-*Ulysses* era there was never any real need for classification. In Class 1 fiction language is a zero quantity, transparent, unseductive, the harmonics of connotation and ambiguity thoroughly damped. The structure has no meaning outside the actions of the plot which sustain it, or which it sustains. Class 1 fiction yearns towards a non-verbal or pre-verbal condition – that of direct presentation of character and actions without the need for the intermediacy of words. Class 1 fiction fulfils its end when transposed to the cinema screen, and many Class 1 novels are better as films than as verbal constructs.

In Class 2 fiction, on the other hand, the opacity of language is exploited, structure may have a significance apart from mere plot, and adaptation to a visual medium invariably conveys little of the essence of the work. If Class 1 fiction is close to film, Class 2 fiction is close to music. The fiction sold in drugstores nearly always belongs to Class 1, and only the adventitious attraction of the violent and/or erotic will permit the admittance of Class 2.

Ulysses is pre-eminently Class 2 fiction. Language is important in itself, and there are structures overlaying the narrative which serve a symbolic end: there is a close Homeric parallel, a compendium of arts and sciences, a textbook of literary techniques, a chromatic spectrum, and a model of the human body. This book was long banned because of its erotic content and dirty language, and it became briefly, before being enshrined as a classic, an honorary Class 1 novel. The same was true of Vladimir Nabokov's *Lolita*, a highly wrought Class 2 artefact and a study of sexual obsession which attracted, but eventually disappointed, the non-literary.

Both these books were filmed, and filmed intelligently, but it was totally impossible to transfer their Class 2 qualities to the screen. In *Ulysses* the symbolism disappeared; in *Lolita* the linguistic obsession which matched the sexual could have no place. Leopold Bloom was not a modern Odysseus, and Humbert Humbert was an ordinary man with a kink. In Nabokov's novel, moreover, we are intended to have doubts as to whether Clare Quilty exists or is merely a projection of the narrator's jealous obsessions. His name is made out of the phrase *Qu'il t'y mène*, and in the murder scene, which is more phantasmagoric than realistic, we suspect the identification of Humbert and Quilty when we read: 'I rolled over him. We rolled over me. They rolled over him. We rolled over us.' But in Stanley Kubrick's film Quilty was disjunct enough and was played by Peter Sellers.

Kubrick filmed a novel of my own which technically has to be assigned to Class 2. This is a study of juvenile violence with a surrealistic-seeming title – *A Clockwork Orange*. To encourage a reader to enjoy the representation of violence is probably immoral and certainly has nothing to do with art. I invented a kind of juvenile argot with a heavy Slav vocabulary which was intended to obscure what it described. In struggling with the language the reader responds to rape and mayhem as it were laterally: he cannot well see what is going on, and, by the time he has disentangled the referents from the strange words, the violence is over. As the theme of the novel is the brainwashing of criminal youth, the structure itself is a device of brainwashing, or certainly conditioning: the reader is intended subliminally to absorb a minimal Russian vocabulary in a carefully devised programme. The peculiar nature of Russian is also intended to condition the images. Russian calls both foot and leg *noga* and both hand and arm *ruka* (very Oriental in this) and when the narrator talks of his rooker or noga we are not sure what he means. The film could do little with the language, and the cinematic art of a permissive age insisted on the candid presentation of violence. I have spent a good deal of time in the last ten years defending myself against charges of incitations to violence levelled by people who, reading the book after seeing the film, used the book as a mere memorandum of what they considered the primary artistic experience.

It is curious that three Class 2 novels – *Ulysses, Lolita* and *A Clockwork Orange* – should, if we use the term in its wider sense, be temporarily adjudged pornographic, since the Class 2 novelist is more concerned with art than moving the reader's flesh. James Joyce, in the persona of Stephen Dedalus, laid down an aesthetic which distinguished between proper and improper art. Improper art is either pornographic or didactic: proper art is static. One can diagrammatize this concept as a continuum, with the pornographic at one end, the didactic at the other, and the static attempting to maintain a middle position. The artist is always in danger of moving from his static posture and embracing either the pornographic or the didactic. If the two ends of the continuum are joined, making a cycloid, then the didactic and the pornographic meet. In a great deal of Class 1 fiction the didactic justifies the pornographic. Indeed, the best-selling formula for our times insists on the combination of frank sex and technical information. The reader enjoys the sex, and, if he feels any shame in this, it can dissolve in a sense of virtue that he is learning how an airport is run, or a bank, or the White House, or a nuclear installation. In Class 2 fiction sexual or aggressive emotions may be aroused, but their arousal and purgation are subordinate to the total structure. In true pornography the pornograph – book or picture – is a mere device for procuring discharge. Very little Class 1 fiction is pornographic in this sense, but titillation is an avowed aim, as is the conveying of information.

André Gide called pornography one-handed literature. He could have said the same of an instruction manual (aptly named) – a cookbook, for example, in which the learner holds the book in his left hand and stirs a sauce with his right. Class 2 writing is two-handed. It also addresses neither the body nor the brain but the imagination. And yet, as the now forgotten scandals of *Ulysses* and *Lolita* show, the mere fact that the most refined art has, like unrefined art, to gain its raw material from the world of fleshly enactments shows that there is an element of corruptibility in the novel that does not exist in music.

The novelist, of whichever class, is tied to the representation of the real world, and the materials it offers are limited: they are mostly what the pornographer and the propagandist exploit. There can be very little fiction without sex, aggression, and various kinds of bigotry and dementia. Any serious literary artist envies music, which has an apparently self-referring language, cannot preach or inform, and totally identifies form and content. The message of music is itself, its narrative is its structure, and it cannot be either pornographic or didactic without the arbitrary addition of a verbal programme. But words can never be freed of their marketplace denotations (the marketplace being also the brothel and the political forum) and the subject matter of fiction is the marketplace. The Class 2 novelist can hope to transcend his subject matter only by concentrating on form. But if he concentrates too much on form he ceases to be a novelist.

The novelist can, unfortunately, learn very little from music, but he can meet music in an area where concerns of structure themselves provide a subject matter. If it is possible to present human action in such a way that the semantic values of the outside world barely intrude, then we can have a kind of fiction as close to music as it is possible to reach. If fictional characters can obey a pattern, and yet seem to possess full autonomy of thought and action, then a kind of fictional music is being played. In *Ulysses* the characters obey an imposed pattern derived from Homer's *Odyssey*, and their acts and thoughts are controlled by an imposed pattern of symbols. Bloom's interior monologues are directed by the structure, and yet he appears to have free will.

The 'structuralist' approach to literature is a fairly new discipline, deriving from Ferdinand de Saussure's theory of language and the anthropological researches of Claude Lévi-Strauss. Man is a culture-making animal, and culture depends on systems of signs, the most important of which is speech and its codification in script. The ability to create such systems depends on a peculiar faculty of the human brain, which is able to select arbitrarily elements out of the continuum of sense data and use them as signs. Signs have cultural validity only when they can be opposed to other signs. In speech we have contrasted phonemes. In the spectrum colours merge into a continuum, but our culture is able to oppose, for instance, green and red in traffic signals. Out of the sound continuum are created those oppositions which provide the tensions and resolutions of music. It is possible to approach literature, as music, through the opposed signs which make up an artistic structure. It is probable that the literary artist creates his art out of a structure-making impulse which has only secondarily a connection with marketplace meanings and judgements.

It is, in fact, important to distinguish between signs as a closed system and signs with a lexical significance. The study of meaning is called semantics, the study of signs is called semiology, and the two are not cognate disciplines. Semantics has always been an imprecise science; to discover meaning is to be involved in an inquiry into the whole of a culture. It is a good deal easier to be concerned with semiotic structures. In studying a Shakespeare sonnet, for instance, it is easier to explicate the pattern of rhymes and stresses than to paraphrase the poem's emotional and intellectual content. The great complaint levelled at the structuralist approach to literature has been that it ignores meaning and studies patterns of imagery and prosody. The approach, one might say, is more suited to music than to literature, for in music there is nothing but signs, and what the signs mean is of little importance.

Without the French semiologists to guide us, we have always been aware that there were certain kinds of fiction which depended more on structure, on the arrangement of signs, than on the statement of new truths about man or society. That once very popular branch of Class 1 fiction, the detective story, depended on the propounding of a riddle and its solution through a reading of the signs. T. S. Eliot wished, as I have said, to attempt a serious study of the genre, but evidently he did not know how to relate it to the rest of literature. It seems to touch the fringes of Class 2 fiction in its concern with structure if not with language, and in a categorization which has nothing to do with value judgements it seems to justify the attraction it has always held for intellectuals. In the writings of the structuralist Roland Barthes, Agatha Christie's name appears more than that of Racine or Shakespeare. A newer category of Class 1 fiction, the science fiction novel or novel of alternative worlds, is concerned with setting up an imaginary social structure whose rationale does not reflect that of our own society. This, like the detective story, is a kind of structuralism, a liberation from marketplace meanings.

I propose in the next chapter to examine with the reader a novel of my own, which was not well understood when it first appeared. Now, ten years after publication, there is a public for it, but the book itself has disappeared from the market. It is not quite a detective story and not quite science fiction, though it is based on a riddle and presents an imaginary society animated by impulses which are not quite the same as ours. It is the kind of novel which might well be written by a musician who had read Claude Lévi-Strauss.

IO
Oedipus Wrecks

In Ford's *'Tis Pity She's a Whore* and Shelley's *The Cenci*, the theme of incest is presented as a ghastly crime against man and nature, material for the grimmest tragedy. The taboo placed on what the Anglo-Saxon bishop Wulfstan called *siblegeru*, or lying with one's sib, is one that not even a rational age cares to question too closely. Inbreeding, say the eugenicists, weakens the stock, but that is too recent a discovery to explain the ferocity with which the prohibition has been enforced in most societies from the earliest times. The rationale of the ban on endogamy, or marrying within one's own social group or family or tribe, can only be presented in terms of the territorial imperative – the need to protect land through alliances, expressed in a law of exogamy. In ancient Egypt, which was powerful and stable and had no enemies, incest was not merely permitted but was mandatory in the royal house. Monarchical Europe, on the other hand, protected territory through foreign alliances confirmed by royal marriages or high-class exogamy. From ancient Greece on, incest became the most terrible of crimes because it compromised the security of the state. The legend of Oedipus, who brought plague and famine to Thebes through unwittingly marrying his own mother, is still the most potent and terrible of our myths. Freud interpreted the legend in terms of fear of the revenge of the castrating father, enraged by filial poaching on his sexual territory, and turned us all into little Oedipuses. He uncovered the main cause of our continued fascination with incest. It is evidently desirable, else it would not be banned.

In his inaugural lecture at the University of Paris, when assuming the chair of anthropology, Claude Lévi-Strauss examined the myth of Oedipus from a structuralist angle. He noted that before committing the deadly act Oedipus was forced to answer a riddle propounded by the Sphinx, a creature half-lion half-woman and, in some effigies, winged. If Oedipus had not been able to answer the riddle, the Sphinx would have devoured him as she had devoured countless others. What interested Lévi-Strauss about the collocation of a riddle (usually asked by a talking animal) and incest was that it was not unique to the Greek legend. Among the Algonquin Indians of North America there were legends which presented the same collocation. Clearly, there was no question of cultural transmission from East to West, so it had to be assumed that the incest/riddle structure was built into certain cultures and was an emanation of human need. He told one story. In an Algonquin tribe a girl accuses her brother of coming to her tent and attempting sexual relations with her. The incest taboo is powerful in the tribe, and the brother is appalled at the very suggestion. There is only one explanation for her allegation, and he finds it: a boy who is exactly his double comes to her tent and tries to rape her. Enraged, the brother kills the boy and disposes of the body. Then he discovers that the boy was the son of a powerful sorceress who has talking owls. The mother comes looking for her son, and the brother has to pretend to be that son to allay an obvious suspicion – that he himself is the boy's murderer. The mother is doubtful. The only way in which the brother can convince her that he is really her son is to marry the girl. The incest taboo being so powerful, he will not do this if he is really, as she suspects, the brother. But he marries his own sister and seems to quell her suspicion. She is not satisfied, however, and sets her talking owls on him. They ask riddles, and if he gives the right answer she will know that incest has been committed and that she has her son's murderer in her power. The brother and sister escape from the situation and are transformed into the sun and moon in eclipse.

In this legend there seemed to me to be material for a novel. While working it up in my mind I happened to come across a curious anticipation of the structuralist approach to incest in the novels of Ivy Compton-Burnett. Her novels all seem to have the same title – *A House and its Head, Elders and Betters, Daughters and Sons, Darkness and Day, A Family and a Fortune*: they are, of course, structurally identical – and I cannot remember exactly where she presents the revelation of incest in one of her families (all really the same family). The response to the revelation, I remember, is not one of horror but of cold-blooded reassessment of the changed family structure, children regretting that they have only one grandfather when they were brought up to believe they had two. Rereading *Finnegans Wake* in order to make a reduced version of it, I noted an even closer anticipation of the structural approach to incest. The whole dream which is the book is powered by sin, which sets the world of fallen man spinning, and the sin is the desire to commit incest. Earwicker is in love with his own daughter. *Incest* being too terrible a word to be admitted even in a dream, the term is metathetized to *insect*, which explains both Earwicker's name and the fable of the Ondt and the Gracehoper. I was particularly interested to note that Earwicker's son Shem is prevented from committing incest with his sister by his inability to answer a very easy riddle. He is asked to guess what a particular colour is. The phonemes in its name are described as 'up tightly in the front . . . down again on the loose . . . drim and drumming on her back . . . and a pop from her whistle.' This works out as *heliotrope*. Shem wets his trousers in shame, but urine in the *Wake* is always semen, and the discharge underlines his inability to commit incest: he is doubly freed from the chance of that sin.

To my greatest astonishment, I found that I had anticipated the riddle/incest motif in one of my own books, written long before I had read Lévi-Strauss. The book is a kind of spy novel called *Tremor of Intent*. The spy Hillier is on his last mission. He conceives a fatherly love for a girl, Clara, whose true father is dying. He has received a riddling message from his department in London, and he is not able to solve it. Clara's father dies and she comes sobbing to him. He gives comfort which turns into sexual comfort, and he feels that he is committing a kind of incest. But later he meets her again, this time as a priest, and he realizes that he had mistaken the significance of 'father'. Evidently, there is a fundamental relationship between incest and riddles, but we do not know what it is. It is in the nature of a structure to be as inexplicable as a passage of music.

My structuralist novel is entitled either *MF* or *M/F*. The first form is a pair of initials, the second symbolizes a structure. The Portuguese version of the novel emphasized the latter and filled out the initials to a basic opposition – male/female. I had been in Hollywood some years before starting the book, and William Conrad, the robust actor who played Cannon in the television series, expressed a half-serious desire to make an all-black film on Oedipus, calling it *Mother Fucker*. This suggested the title, but the initials primarily stand for the name of the hero, Miles Faber, a name which combines two main attributes of man – the aggressive and the creative.

My own initials appear on the title page but in one of the two available musical forms – A and B natural. Beginning a scale and beginning an alphabet, it is meant to stand for a structure which is not quite a structure. For neither a scale nor an alphabet is a *significant* structure, it is merely the code out of which significant structures are made. There are two epigraphs which relate respectively to structures and riddles. The first comes from a book on linguistics by the late and regretted Simeon Potter: 'In his *Linguistic Atlas of the United States and Canada* Hans Kurath recognizes no isogloss coincident with the political border along Latitude 49°N.' In other words, the continuity of American English is not halted by a mere political frontier. The opposition Canada/United States is a false, or insignificant, structure. The other epigraph is from the First Folio of *Much Ado About Nothing*: 'Enter Prince, Claudio and Jacke Wilson.' Jacke Wilson, who presumably played Balthazar, was an actor–singer in the Lord Chamberlain's company of players. Jack Wilson is the real name of Anthony Burgess. There is no true riddle here. Either one knows the identification or one does not. The question that ought to be asked is: why did one name change into the other? There is no easy answer.

The action of the first chapter takes place in a bedroom of, inevitably, the Algonquin Hotel on West 44th Street, New York City. I am telling the reader that he is on Algonquin territory, but also Iroquois, since the Iroquois Hotel is a few blocks away. Algonquin/Iroquois is a meaningful opposition, far more than United States/Canada, for the two Indian nations had different cultures and languages and they fought each other. The story to come is based on an Algonquin legend, hence the choice of one hotel rather than the other. Miles Faber, a young man not yet come of age, meets the family lawyer Loewe in his bedroom. He is highly strung and a heavy smoker, and the cigarettes he prefers are a Korean brand, Sinjantin. This will have meaning later. Miles has been sent down from his college in Massachusetts for fornicating in the open air in public: the act is taken by his fellow-students as a sign standing for undifferentiated protest. His English professor, Keteki (Sanskrit for riddle), quoted in class from a certain Fenwick's diary for the year 1596. Fenwick saw a play and says of it: 'Gold gold and even titularly so.' What, asks Keteki, was the name of the play? He will give twenty dollars to the student who can give the most plausible answer. Miles recollects that *fenek* is the Maltese word for rabbit, and thinks that Fenwick might have anglicized his Maltese name, Fenek being a not uncommon surname in Malta. The Maltese word *jew* stands for the conjunction *or*. *Or* in French means gold. The play was probably *The Jew of Malta*. Miles wins the twenty dollars and gets drunk on it. He meets a lady who persuades him to copulate with her in public. Thus he is thrown out of his college.

Miles clearly has a mad Oedipal talent. He can answer riddles and solve crosswords with no trouble. He makes, with the total automatism he gives to smoking, a riddle on the name of the lawyer Loewe:

> Behold the sheep form side by side
> A Teuton roarer of the pride.

Lo means behold, *ewe* is a sheep, and in German *Loewe* is a lion. Nearly all the people Miles will meet in the course of the narrative will either have animal names or resemble animals. This prefigures a sphingine danger to the young Oedipus. The Sphinx was both human and animal. The talking owls of the sorceress of the Algonquin legend combine a non-human body with a human talent: they are a kind of sphinx. When Keteki asked the riddle in class, Miles answered without hesitation: *keteki* merely means the thing he was asking. When Loewe puts a riddle, or rather a crossword clue, to Miles, Miles knows the answer, but some instinct tells him not to give it.

Miles, having terminated his college career abruptly, wishes to continue his education privately. On the island of Castita in the Caribbean, there are said to be the literary and artistic remains of a certain Sib Legeru (you know what the name means, but Miles does not), a genius whom Professor Keteki knows about and specimens of whose work he has already given to Miles to read. Miles sees in this work a total artistic freedom, an abandonment of form and meaning, a disdain of structure. Miles, being very young, has a negative attitude to structure whether in art or in morality: his *al fresco* fornication was an indication of this. Miles wants Loewe to give him money out of his dead father's estate so that he can make the journey to Castita and study, having first located, Sib Legeru's works. Loewe demurs. Miles has a responsibility to the Faber family, of which he is the only surviving member. His father believed in miscegenation, or exogamy, holding that the future of civilization rested on the mingling of the races. If Miles will not continue his studies he ought to assume the responsibility as head of the Faber family by marrying a Chinese girl named Miss Ang and begetting a mixed progeny. But finally he yields to Miles's entreaty and gives him five hundred dollars. It is now summer; Miles's birthday, when he comes of age, is on Christmas Eve. The money should last him until then and the beginning of his adult responsibilities.

Left alone, Miles turns on the television set. The first channel shows athletes levitating to the music of Johann Strauss. The reader, if not Miles, will find the name Lévi-Strauss charaded there. The next channel has a talk show, with a member of the Nipissing tribe talking of the commercial future of the Indians. The Nipissing people are, Miles knows (he has much useless knowledge, he thinks), members of the great Algonquin family. He then goes to sleep and dreams of an Indian sorceress. He does not see her, but he hears her announced: 'It is she of the koko-koho.' He sees her owls and one of them twitters at him a strange word: *Esa esa*. He wakes up in inexplicable terror. His watch has stopped at 19.17 (the year of the birth of Jack Wilson). He dials the telephone for the time but remembers the wrong dialling formula. ULCERSS gives him no reply. He recollects that that is the Los Angeles formula; for New York he must dial NERVOUS. Time is as painful a structure as a '*Mauer* or a parallel or a taxonomy'. The *Mauer* divides Berlin, the parallel divides

Canada and the United States, though not the Indians, who accept different divisions. The taxonomy, or arranging of the world into categories, is painful to him because he desires total freedom, the collapse of structures. But he cannot escape from structures as easily as he thinks.

He goes for a meal and hears the waitresses shouting their orders. He does not know that they are announcing, in acrostic form, the great Oedipal sin: 'Indiana (or Illinois) nutbake. Chuffed eggs. Saffron toast. Whiting in tarragon, hot. Michigan (or Missouri) oyster-stew. Tenderloin. Hash, egg. Ribs.' He hears a male voice dictating into a tape recorder details of the structural difference between the instant soup of American kitchens and the soup of French kitchens where the pot has bubbled non-stop for four centuries. The French soup, says the voice, is a synchronic metaphor of the diachronic: it turns time into space, history into a single edible plateful. Miles, leaving, sees an old crippled man, with a false hand and crutches, who nods at him 'in a kind of shy confidence'. From his accent he seems French but he does not look French (we are not told how not). The name on the case which contains his recording spools is Z. Fonanta. Miles does not know the meaning of this, but the reader, presumably, does: *Zoon Fonanta* is Greek for talking animal. Traditionally it means man, but it must mean more in an Oedipal story. Miles has also failed to note the significance of the name of a soft drink he has taken with his dinner: Koko-Koho. This name is the Algonquinian for owl. The bottle itself is in the rough shape of an owl, but the owl is comic, passive, a mere vessel. Owls, birds in general, are not to be feared.

When Miles returns to his hotel to get his bag and then leave for the airport (there is a 2200 Air Carib flight for Grencijta – 'Big Town' – capital of Castita), he finds Loewe back in his room with a hired thug. Miles is to be prevented from leaving right away. There are reasons, newly recalled by Loewe, confirmed by a lawyer in Miami, Mr Pardaleos (leopard, another animal, this time Greek), for delaying his departure. The reasons are not given. Loewe asks for the return of the five hundred dollars. But Miles is not having this. He leaves and his leaving is not seriously opposed: this puzzles him. In the hotel lobby he sees a young man in levis carrying a wreath (*Strauss* in German). An airport limousine is waiting. Two of the air companies it serves are plausible enough – Air Carib, Udara Indonesia (*udara* means air) – but the third is impossible: Loftsax. A company called Loftsax would have to have existed before the Norman Conquest.

Miles is not taken to the airport. Instead he is made to alight by two more thugs, presumably sent by Loewe, and his money is taken from him except for enough to buy a beer. He is on Broadway, outside a cinema which announces *La Forma de la Espada* (the name of an unfilmed story by Borges, another form of Burgess). He has to get money somehow, so he offers himself as a gigolo to a woman met in a bar. Her name is Irma (no animal connection), and she lives on multiple alimony. In her flat Miles finds a cutting from *Seee* (impossible orthography there only to fulfil a mandatory four-letter structure), the review of a novel called *Bub Boy*. The authoress is Carlotta Tukang. There is a photograph of her, and Miles recognizes his sexual partner of the previous night. That the encounter might have been incestuous does not occur to Miles, but the review of another book, *The President's Nephews* (taking the term nepotism literally), ought to worry him: the author's name is Blutschande, German for incest. Miles gets money, though only enough to take him as far as Miami on a pluribus of Unum Airline. On the plane he dreams of Miss Emmett, his old nanny, and the fantasy does not, though its symbols ought to, disclose that she is really what her name means – an ant. He remembers her singing a song, her only one – 'You will be my summer queen'. Obligingly the author quotes the tune in a footnote. There will be other tunes – a hymn, a state anthem, a wedding march – and they will all be variants of this tune. Just before reaching Miami Miles discovers that an agent of Mr Pardaleos has been quietly accompanying him on the flight. Bafflingly, this man, in black for a colleague's funeral, is also a policeman who has to arrest a certain Guzman at Miami airport.

Mr Pardaleos, a Greek, is waiting for Miles in the airport restaurant, the Savarin. The cuisine, in real life, is detestable, the name mockery. But in the narrative an onomastic magic converts the food into an epicure's dream, and Pardaleos eats heartily of it. He explains to Miles why he must not go at once to Castita. He has a sister there, whose existence has up till now been kept from him, for a demented reason of his dead father. His father committed incest with his own sister, Miles's mother–aunt (the cop in black is probably called Hamnet or Hammett), and he feared that the incestuous urge might run in the family. If Miles meets his sister, he may be tempted to repeat the paternal crime. Therefore he must wait a few days in Miami. The sister, with her old nanny or governess, is shortly to go to France (possibly to study *structuralisme*): in the meantime, by a most astonishing coincidence, she is still residing on the very island whither Miles aims to travel. Miles is horrified and shocked by these revelations. Everything is being placed in the way of his simple and chaste desire (Castita means chastity) to further his studies. A feeble attempt is made in the airport washroom to hold him back by another pair of thugs, but Guzman has just been arrested and, by pretending to be Guzman, Miles is able to join the charter flight on which Guzman was attempting to get out of America. This flight is bound for Ojeda, another fictitious Caribbean island, and in Ojeda Miles manages to find a berth as cook on a Bermuda cutter called the *Zagadka* (Russian for a riddle), owned by two homosexual Americans. They are willing to voyage to Grencijta, one place being as good or bad as another. A great storm hits them, Miles falls and knocks himself out, surrounded by the scattered contents of a nautical dictionary. Regarded as a Jonah by the Americans, he becomes a genuine Jonah, sinking into whale-belly darkness and emerging to engage his serious role – no longer a querulous rebel but a mature mythic character. He is ready to confront (though he does not know this) the destiny that the mysterious engines of the incest/riddle structure are about to impose on him.

It is a festal day in Grencijta, and there is a procession in honour of the island's matron saint, Euphorbia, martyred under Domitian. (Domitian, according to Robert Graves, is the beast figured in the 666 of Revelations: DCLXVI, meaning Domitianus Caesar Legatos Christi Violenter Interfecit.) A choral hymn gives Miles, and ourselves, some notion of the phonetic structure of the Castitan language: *Senta Euphorbia/ Vijula vijulata/ Ruza inspijnata.* . . It is a Romance language in which the original Latin vowels have been raised to the limit: they are trying to break out of their vocalic bounds and become consonants. The procession is both religious and secular. It ends with a circus parade, and Miles learns that a travelling circus is at present on the island. Elefanta's or Fonanta's or Bonanza's or Atlanta's Circus: he finds the name unclear. The cheering crowd grows silent at the appearance of a strange woman in the procession – tall, gaunt, a kind of sorceress surrounded by birds screaming human language (mynahs, parrots, starlings, but no owls). She seems to look at Miles with a kind of angry recognition. He will discover why later.

Meanwhile, needing money, he earns it by setting himself up as Mr Memory Junior, offering to answer any question put by the holiday crowd. A boy quietly asks him the date of the founding of the multiracial University College of Salisbury, Rhodesia, as it then was, but Miles does not know the answer. He pretends to the crowd that the question put was really: When was the first public showing of television? The answer to this he knows: 13 July 1930, in England, by the Baird process. What he does not know is that that date is also the date of the founding of the Rhodesian college. He is being used by forces unknown. The Sphinx is due to appear, and she appears in male form, that of an old cripple whose body has been deformed into the caricature of a lion. The questions have turned to riddles (most of them Maltese), but the lionman has made up one of his own:

> Throatdoor, tongueback, nose and teeth
> Spell a heavenblack hell beneath.
> Engage warily, young men,
> Lest it prove a lion's den.

Miles knows the answer at once (*cunt*) but will not give it. It would be uttering an obscenity in public on an island whose name means chastity. He does not know the real reason for not answering.

A time of rest now, in a small hotel, the Batavia, run by a lady from the opposed Indies, an Indonesian who smokes a brand of cigarettes called Dji Sam Soe. Miles remembers that he has no more Sinjantin (stolen by the thugs of the airport bus) and this deprivation blinds him to a structural truth which casts doubt on the reality of the story of which he is a part. He notes the decor of the lobby, the garden without, a group of cardplayers, and hears a girl ask on the telephone for the number 113 and Mr R. J. Wilkinson. He does not see the connection between these things. R. J. Wilkinson compiled a classic dictionary – Malay (or Indonesian) – English – and the entire scene is made out of the words on page 113 of that work. In his bedroom he finds a rulebook for association football and a referee's whistle, presumably left behind by an absentminded visiting referee. Some instinct tells him to wear the whistle round his neck, under his shirt, as a talisman. He is, without knowing it, becoming mature: a referee's whistle symbolizes rules, fair play, a rigid closed structure. He sleeps, and goes down to hear two things from the Indonesian lady who owns the hotel. He is invited to dinner at the Pepeghelju (parrot: talking bird) by a certain Dr Gonzi (the name is not significant: it is merely that of the Archbishop of Malta, a kind of Castita, at the time when, in Malta, I was writing the novel). He is asked to admire the conciseness of the Malay or Indonesian language. *Tulat tukang tuil* means: The day after the day after tomorrow the skilled workman will carry a burden over his shoulder on a stick with a stick over the other shoulder to support it. *Tulat* sounds like *too late*, *tuil* like *too ill*. *Tukang* means the same as Faber, his own name. He ought to have a good reason for remembering that word, but there are too many other things crowding in on him.

The Pepeghelju restaurant has a talking parrot in its garden: it speaks with the accent of New South Wales. Dr Gonzi awaits him: he is the lionman, the Sphinx, and he is already drunk. He is suicidally depressed. A scholar, expert on Bishop Berkeley, he has been offered a post in the freak show of the visiting circus. He wants to die, but he would prefer to hang for murder than take his own life. He proposes asking Miles a riddle. He does not think Miles will be able to answer it. He will shoot Miles and then be arrested for murder. He certainly has a gun: he brandishes it. The riddle is not really much more than a silly word puzzle:

> Move and my own self enclose
> A land above the deeper snows.

Miles at once sees what it means – the lionman's own name: to move is to go, New Zealand or NZ is the land meant, *my own self* is I. But he will not answer. Gonzi's gun arm is drunkenly unsteady, and it is moreover deflected by the parrot's sudden whistle. Miles runs, remembers his own whistle, uses it loudly to bring the police. Gonzi searches for him, staggering and cursing. But a police van arrives and takes Miles to the station.

There, to his astonishment, he finds himself treated as a criminal. He is recognized as a young man who has already caused disturbance in the city. His belongings are examined, and the police inspector makes a suspicious structure out of certain vocables: Tu kang sin jan tin jee sam soo. Miles feels that, though he has come West, he is being dragged East, probably to marry Miss Ang. For the first time he recognizes dimly that he is contained in a structure he does not understand and which he cannot control. When told that his real name is Llew, he suspects that he must have a double. This is confirmed when Mr Dunkel, manager of the visiting circus, is sent for. Llew has been causing stupid juvenile trouble in the town. Miles, whom Dunkel without hesitation takes for Llew, is to be confined in the caravan which he shares with his mother on the circus site outside the city.

And so Miles comes face to face with his double. Llew, a young Welshman, is an appalling personage, crude, vulgar, given to pornography, pop music, as much raw sex as he can get. Are they perhaps sundered twins? Impossible. Llew's mother is the bird queen of the circus. She is named Aderyn, Welsh for bird. She has a whole spectrum of hawks and the talking birds Miles has already seen and heard. Her act is magical, her birds are totally in her control. Llew, a circus boy, has failed at the various circus tasks given to him, but now he suggests that he and Miles work out an act whose success will depend on Miles disguising himself in real life, so that identity can be exploited in the closed structure of the circus. Miles regards himself as the primal owner of a particular face and body and refuses hotly. They part with hard words.

The following day Miles begins his search for the literary and artistic remains of Sib Legeru. The President of Castita is shot at, and Miles suspects Dr Gonzi. In a bar he meets, to his overwhelming surprise, his old nanny Miss Emmett: she is not drinking but buying a packet of Honeydew cigarettes (in conformity

with her ant identity). She has, as she always had, a pair of
scissors dangling from her waist. Though not herself Welsh, in
the Welsh manner she makes *scissors* a dual word, using a singular
article with it. Miles discovers that she is here with his sister
Catherine. At last he meets his sister, an ugly and slovenly girl
who has been mentally ill. Their father, apparently, made an
incestuous attack on her, and Miss Emmett repulsed him with
her ever-present scissors. The possibility of Miles's wishing himself to commit incest with her is infinitely remote: she is physically repellent as well as selfish and stupid. But he agrees to
sacramentalize their meeting and his reunion with Miss Emmett
by sharing a meal. They offer only sugary things; he goes out to
buy wine and a piece of beef. While shopping, he finds a shop
which sells Sinjantin cigarettes and also has, hanging on a nail,
the key to the shed where the Sib Legeru treasures are stored.
The shed is on the street where Catherine and Miss Emmett are
lodged (Indovinella Street: I need not translate), but its exact
whereabouts are unsure. Miles cooks dinner. Miss Emmett is
unused to the thick dark wine he serves and goes to sleep in the
kitchen, but not before she has told him that the shed is here,
in the garden, and is loaded with old papers and other rubbish.

Nearly fainting with excitement, Miles opens the shed and is
overwhelmed with what he finds – paintings with inexplicable
patterns, a novel in which there is no covenant, either of character identity or continuity of action, with the reader, a poem
which enchants Miles:

> London Figaro infra pound
> Threejoint dackdiddy Solomon
> Delay delay thou Gabriel hound
> Mucklewrath IHS brilliging on
> Ants alley jackalent Meckerbound
> Skysent stone threw sinkiss black
> And caged Cardinal Mabinogion
> Though M is NN copied slack
> A freehand onestroke perfect round
> Took that bony face aback!

He thinks he has at last met total artistic liberation from the
meanings of the marketplace. His reading is interrupted by
screams from within the house. He rushes there. Miss Emmett

is still asleep. Upstairs in her bedroom Catherine is fighting off an attempted rape by Llew. Llew, desisting for a moment, says, reasonably enough, that he was in the street below and she at the window: she called him in, saying it was time for bed. Catherine is aghast at the apparition of a double Miles and near-hysterical at her near-deflowering. She calls Miss Emmett out of her sleep.

Miss Emmett appears with her scissors. Llew makes for the open window. Miles notes that, in a combined Anglo-Welsh structure, three duals come together: scissors, ballocks, trousers. Llew falls out of the window and cracks his skull on a broken birdbath in the garden. Miles lugs the body to the shed where the Sib Legeru treasures await his reperusal. There is danger now. Aderyn will be looking for her son. Miles, Catherine and Miss Emmett must leave the island at once, but a television announcement discloses the shutting of all ports until the attempted assassin of the President is apprehended. Miles must pretend to be the dead Llew: he has enough acting ability to go through with the impersonation, or so he hopes. Catherine must go to the police and inform them that the would-be assassin is Dr Gonzi: this means telling of Gonzi's death urge; it means also the solving of the silly word puzzle.

The story now follows the Algonquin legend pretty closely. Aderyn has her suspicions. Miles, as Llew, drives her to an appointment with an oculist: she has been scratched in the eye by one of her hawks (transference of Oedipus's punishment). He goes to see his sister to find out if there has been any response from the police, also to see how Miss Emmett, who has gone to sleep again and will not wake up, is getting on. Aderyn pursues him. In his Llew persona Miles has to say that this is the girl he loves and wishes to marry. Aderyn agrees to the marriage almost at once, and it is arranged to take place that very night in the circus ring after the performance. All the clowns are crypto-theologians, some of them in full orders: no difficulty in finding an officiating priest or pastor.

And now there appears the man whom Miles had previously heard dictating into a recorder in a New York eating house. Catherine knows him – Dr Fonanta. She was sent to this island to be placed under his care. He specializes in mental disorders

relating to passive or active involvement in the incestuous act.
He seems, like Lévi-Strauss himself, to know all the traditional
concomitants of a coming incestuous marriage. 'A pity there'll
be no eclipse tonight. I gather there'll be fireworks, though.
There's probably some rotting meat about somewhere.' There is
too – that roast beef of last night. Miles hurls it on its china dish
into the garden. The putrefying meat will join the economy of
nature; the shards of broken plate will be the useless remnants
of an aspect of human culture. But Dr Fonanta means something
else – the corpse of Llew.

He is disclosed, during the bizarre wedding ceremony, as the
owner of the circus. He is also a bad poet. Miles distractedly
suspects that he cannot, despite his accent, be really French: one
of his poems collates roast pork and apple sauce – synchronic
sweet and savoury inadmissible, according to the structuralists
of Paris, in the Western cuisine. After the ceremony he makes
sure that Miles and Catherine are safely bedded. Now comes the
act of incest. Miles knows he is being watched and listened to:
the bedroom chosen for them is full of electronic devices. He
spurts seed, but not into his sister. Was this properly an incestuous act? The *vas muliere* has been not a depository for the
semen of incestuous generation but a mere temporary engine of
stimulation. Aderyn is still not convinced that this is her own
son. He must be given a final examination, made to submit to
the riddling birds. And now Miles conceives a suspicion so intense as to amount to a conviction.

Llew was never Aderyn's true son, merely an adopted one. He
was born, he discovers, on Christmas Eve, Miles's own birthday.
Llew may mean lion in Welsh, but it is probably part of a
palinlogue – Nowell, a form of Noel which, backwards, is Leon,
another lion. Aderyn is shaken at the rupturing of a secret, but
she goes ahead with her magic. A cockatoo is to ask a riddle. If
Llew–Miles gets the answer wrong his eyes will be torn out by
the hawks. The riddle is:

> Who was the final final, say,
> That was put back but had his day?

There are two opposed answers, both equally valid. One is *God*,
which is *dog* backwards (every dog has his day), the final final,

the ultimate reality. But the opposed ultimate reality is *devil*, *lived* backwards: if you have lived you have had your day. Whichever answer Miles gives will be the wrong one. He gives it, and the hawks swoop to the tearing. Then he remembers his referee's whistle, blasts it at the birds, which, in their confusion, turn on their mistress. The true confirmatory answer should have been: *Mam mam I'm frightened take them away mam.*

Dr Fonanta clears everything up. The following morning Catherine and Miss Emmett are able to leave the island. Dr Gonzi has been shot by the police. Llew's body has been quietly buried. Llew was Miles's sundered twin, no magical coincidence. Dr Fonanta is Miles's grandfather. His initials, like his grandson's, are M. F., and they stand also for his own act of incest – with his mother. By forcing Miles and his sister into an incestuous situation, instead of merely leaving it to chance and perverse nature, the strange spell cast on the Faber family has at last been exorcised. Miles will marry Miss Ang. Miles wonders if perhaps the sexual encounter with Carlotta Tukang was not incestuous. His mother may not after all have died, she may be his mother, Tukang means Faber, Miles answered Keteki's riddle correctly (Keteki, now he comes to think of it, had the look of an owl). But Dr Fonanta, or Miles Faber, reassures him. Tukang is a deformation of Toucan, a bird name. This means that Miles got the classroom riddle wrong: whatever the play was, it was not *The Jew of Malta*. As for the works of Sib Legeru, there was no such person. *Siblegeru* means what it meant to Bishop Wulfstan; those works are aspects of the therapy of Dr Fonanta's patients. They are not denials of structure, they are confirmations of taxonomic structures, though these are essentially false structures. They are based on the alphabetic arrangement of words (like the lobby of the Batavia Hotel), or on word transformation games, like *bread broad brood blood blond bland*. The stupidity of so-called total freedom in art, as in life, is best exemplified in a musical score of Sib Legeru's: in it a bassoon is made to go down to a low F sharp, a note impossible on the instrument.

Miles ends his story in Bracciano, north of Rome. He ends it there because I ended it there, having just escaped from Malta. He is married to Miss Ang, but they cannot have children. They have adopted children, and these may well intermarry, committing merely nominal incest. Miles Faber now reveals that he is black, though the reader may have, certainly has indeed, taken him for white. If he is black other characters are black too. The reader must reread, adjusting colours as he does. But the colour does not matter. Black/white is an unfruitful opposition, quite unlike male/female. As for the story, 'the main structure is solidly true, but would it matter much if it weren't? Those Sinjantin cigarettes have least of all to do with the structure, yet in a sense they're the truest thing about the whole narrative.' The cigarettes exist: I have a half-empty packet before me as I write. The reader may not believe me, but it is true. What, however, is truth? All we have is structures.

I cannot really apologize for summarizing the plot of my little structuralist novel at such length. We are living in an age when books go so rapidly out of print that it is of little use to refer the reader to a work published as long ago as 1971. The pity is that not many were ready for the book when it appeared: the principles of structuralism had not yet been widely diffused. There is a generation ready now, I think, but the unsold copies of *MF* or *M/F* have long been pulped. There is, however, another reason for my summary. The plot seems totally unsuitable for a work of orthodox fiction, and it can only be made acceptable by being dressed up, as I dressed it up, in the trappings of an almost popular novel – plausible, as opposed to structural, motivations; realistic dialogue; comfortingly familiar details from the known twentieth-century world. As a bare skeleton, the story discloses all the elements of a closed structure, like a piece of music, with a labyrinth of logic that does not apply to a world where incest is just a pleasantly horrible perversion and not an aberration to be considered amorally, with reference to riddles and talking animals. Why a riddle put by a being half-animal half-human should be associated with the act of incest, we cannot say. My novel defers to the reader's need of a rational explanation by saying something like 'It is dangerous to question the mysteries of natural order, which are symbolized in riddles', but that is no answer. Questions about these structural relations are as meaningless as attempts to find out the meaning of a fugue or a sonata.

One of the laws about incest put forward by Lévi-Strauss has not, I think, found a place here. Because the oracle said that

Oedipus would commit parricide and incest in Thebes, he was sent as a child to Corinth. But he got to Thebes. 'The thing you do,' says the great French structuralist, 'to avoid committing incest is the very thing that will lead you to it.' (This is a basic law which applies to other forbidden acts as presented in legend or literature.) My not quite (after all) Oedipal hero (the true Oedipal hero appears very belatedly) is sent to commit incest, and the apparent obstacles put in his way – they are all feeble and avoidable – are there to whet his desire to get to the place where incest will be committed. The whole thing seems to be rigged not by the mysterious engines of myth, but by a man who knows about myths, is quite cold-blooded in his engineering, but is superstitious in his belief that a curse on the house of Faber must be broken by control of the very means that brought the curse about. But he too is enclosed in myth.

I do not think it is possible to write many novels of this kind, but I do believe, and I think the little book proves it, that it is possible to juggle with the free will of fictional characters and the predestination of an imposed structure. This is, after all, the manner of music, in which the component strands seem to go their own way but are locked in a preconceived pattern. There may be a theological conclusion to be drawn from this, and all art may be in the service of a theological truth about the mere illusion of free will, but I refuse to venture too deeply into the matter. It is enough to get on with the task of creating art without asking why one is doing it.

11
Bonaparte in E Flat

Immediately after publishing *MF* or *M/F* I started work on a more ambitious fictional structure. This was *Napoleon Symphony*. As the title *MF* came out of Hollywood, the idea of a novel on Napoleon was pushed to realization by a film director who had forsaken Hollywood to work in England. This director wished to make a Napoleon film which should encompass the Corsican's entire career, and not at any extravagant length. He needed a structure to work with, and I knew that I myself could only produce the protomorph of a novel which might supply such a structure by drawing on Beethoven's 'Eroica' Symphony. I had in mind a book of not much more than 100,000 words, divided into four sections corresponding to Beethoven's four movements. The correspondence should extend to duration as well as form and tempo. Thus, if the last section of the novel was to be about eighty pages long, the penultimate section could not be more than about thirty – this indicating roughly the proportion in playing time between Beethoven's scherzo and his finale. Tempo was to be no mere metaphor. Some kinds of prose are speedier than others, and it seemed to me possible to produce an allegro pace in my first movement and an adagio in my second. Form was a more difficult matter. It was wiser to think of the distribution of material first, what was to go into which movement.

This is how I roughly worked it out. The opening allegro should take Bonaparte from his early Italian triumphs to his crowning as Emperor – about 120 pages of print, meaning about 100 of typescript. In his marcia funebre Beethoven has already killed and buried his great man. I could not do this, but I could match defeat and the mere memory of past triumphs to the

funereal tempo. In the scherzo Beethoven resurrects his hero as
Prometheus. I could do that, but I also had to push on with the
narrative to the final defeat of Waterloo, being forced, by the
scherzo speed, to present this with almost comic, or Keystone
Cops, rapidity. In the final section Napoleon had to be an exile
on St Helena, and also Prometheus with the eagles of disease
pecking his liver. Somehow I had to find the literary equivalent
of a theme and variations. I would solve that problem when I
came to it.

It is always as well, when writing fiction, to begin at the
beginning and shut one's mind entirely to the problems lying
further ahead – including the unthinkable possibility that it
might be beyond one's imaginative and technical capacity to
bring the work to a satisfactory end. Like other writers, I have
begun books which I could not finish. With Napoleon's story I
was at least in the comfortable position of having his biography
to draw on. Indeed, I had little to invent except scenes and
dialogue corresponding to historical fact. The problem was nearly
completely formal: how to make true history fit into musical
patterns.

The first movement of the novel does not begin until some
preliminary material has been presented. Josephine, her lawyer
Calmelet, Tallien and Barras are waiting for Buonaparte (not yet
Bonaparte), as are we. A marriage has been arranged, and the
bridegroom is late. The acting registrar is asleep by the fire, and
his wooden leg is beginning to scorch. The characters fantasize
about the tree from which the leg was taken – the Tree of France,
the source of wood pulp for a new edition of Rousseau or for the
penning of the constitutions of Mirabeau, sawdust to make bread
during the famine riots, truncheons for the police to break riot-
ers' heads. They make up rhymes, warning the reader that verse
will help out prose in the narrative to come. In a symphony the
distinction between prose and verse rhythms is not easy to make,
and this book is a symphony. But the symphony has not yet
begun, and the conductor's baton, that scorching wooden leg,
lies asleep. The pagination, in Roman numerals, is proper to a
preface, not a text. Eventually Buonaparte marches in, bids the
acting registrar awake and take his baton out of the fire, gives
Josephine two sharp love tweaks on the earlobes corresponding

to the two sforzando chords before the double bar at the start of Beethoven's allegro, and cries, like the Joyce of the Sirens or Walther with his Trial Song: 'Begin!' The pagination from now on will be in regular arabic numerals. We go straight into the first movement.

Here comes the major formal problem of the whole conception. Sonata form depends on repetition, and repetition is what neither fictional nor historical narrative can accommodate – at least, not in the literal manner of music. The first section of the novel must have four subsections, corresponding to Beethoven's exposition, development section, recapitulation and coda. In the score Beethoven indicates, in the tradition of all classical symphonists (up to and including Brahms), that the exposition may be repeated. In practice, since the first movement is exceptionally long, this is rarely done. However, there is nothing to stop the score-reader's listening in his skull to the sequence *exposition, first time bars, repeat of exposition, second time bars*. There is likewise nothing to stop my readers from going through the first subsection again. But this conventional or mechanical repetition is not at all the same as structural repetition, whereby the recapitulation substantially restates the exposition with certain elisions, expansions, and unifying key changes. How can the novelist overcome the problem of giving the *effect* of repetition while pushing on with his narrative? Only by echoing situations, phrases, preoccupations and structures already encountered, but in a new context of action.

Thus, my exposition begins with the words 'Germinal in the Year Four' and follows with a passionate interior monologue from Bonaparte on the theme of his love for Josephine. Massena, Augereau, La Harpe and Kilmaine discuss him after a bad breakfast, scoffing ribaldly at his excessive sexuality but conceding his power of military leadership. My recapitulation begins with the words 'Germinal in the Year Seven' and follows with a passionate interior monologue from Bonaparte on the theme of his continuing love, despite her infidelity, for Josephine. As First Consul, presiding over a meeting of the Council, he writes on his order paper *God how much I love you* over and over in total automatism (historical fact). Cambacérès and Lebrun, the other Consuls, discuss him on the way to a good breakfast, considering him not quite human – he has no interest in food and 'swives like a rattlesnake' – but conceding his power of civic leadership.

If Bonaparte, or N, as I call him, is the nucleus of the masculine thematic group we may call the first subject, Josephine is the nucleus of the second, or feminine, subject. Her appearances in the recapitulation correspond in position to her appearances in the exposition, but N appears most, and it is his themes which receive the more vigorous development. Beethoven does little with his own brief second subject.

It is the use of pieces of verse, in the opposed, or sometimes conjoining, styles of the Age of Reason and Age of Romanticism, which can establish *visual* points of reference (as in an orchestral score). Towards the end of the exposition N stands on the plateau of Rivoli. Six lines of heroic couplets, followed by a triplet, represent the plateau, and N's battle plan is outlined in footnotes. The numbers in the text referring to these are not in consecutive order but are fixed like map references. The corresponding verse passage of the recapitulation is not rhymed but blank, and it romantically describes the death of Desaix. Each passage is followed by the prose celebration of a victory, and these victories are the natural culminations of the structures. The technique of the piece of verse with footnotes appears once more, mainly for the sake of formal balance, at the end of the coda. N is crowned Emperor of the French, a conventional Spenserian stanza glorifies him, the footnotes describe in ironical terse prose the tripping over the Empress's train, the Emperor's nodding off and suffering a brief premonitory nightmare.

These formal niceties are perhaps too pedantic to be important. What, to the author at least, seems to be important is the encouragement which the example of the 'Eroica' gives to the speeding up of action, the rapid alternation of scenes (too fast for the cinema), and the change from prose to verse and back in the service of colloquial expansion and narrative concision. Beethoven moves from the aggressive to the lyrical, changes key without warning, shifts from the sharply chordal to the urgently contrapuntal. The reader, aware of the musical provenance of the novel, may be willing to accept contrapuntal ingenuities like the following (the voices are those of N, Josephine, and her children Eugène and Hortense):

O GOD TO THINK THAT ONE TO WHOM I ENTRUSTED MY VERY
INNERMOST HEART IN KEEPING but I swear it is all long over it was
foolish but it is long done I have lived a life of solitary virtue there is
evidence talk to Madame Gohier your whole family is against me they
will say anything I WOULD HAVE DONE BETTER TO LISTEN TO MY
FAMILY A MAN CAN TRUST ONLY HIS KIND O GOD GOD THE TREACHERY
LET ME NEVER TRUST ANY WOMAN AGAIN I WHO SPENT SUCH TRUST
ON A WORTHLESS WORTHLESS *let us speak for our mother let us speak for
ourselves let us be a happy and united family she loves you we love you you
love her* YES EUGENE YOU ARE A BRAVE FINE YOUNG MAN AND YOU
HORTENSE ARE O GOD GOD GOD I was foolish God knows I was foolish
but I learned my lesson long before these calumnies spread

And so on. The passage corresponds roughly to the fugato in
Beethoven's development section. My own development, cover-
ing the Egyptian campaign, the discovery of Josephine's perfidy,
the rapid return to France and the taking over of the government,
is justified in its delirium and hysteria not only by history but by
the very nature of the musical free fantasia.

When the novel first appeared, certain critics sneered at the
obviousness, or banality, of a basic structural opposition. N fears
water, unless it can be tamed into civic fountains; he feels himself
in control of the land. They missed an attempt on my part to
find equivalents for the heroic stability of the home key of E flat
(earth) and the very distant key which begins Beethoven's coda
– that of D flat. The coda begins with N's brooding over the
perfidy of water, the woman element, and an attempt at his
destruction by a dissident bomb immediately follows. If the D
flat of danger can be read as C sharp, it will enable the coda to
find its way back to the opening theme, which contains C sharp,
and a final assertion of triumph. Terrorism, financed by England,
ruler of the perfidious element, can be converted into the police
rigour of a tyranny: the enemy's D flat becomes N's C sharp,
which will take him, through home-associated keys, to the E flat
of his coronation. This is probably too fanciful. Give us, for
God's sake, a plain read.

Unplain readers may care to notice that in this same coda,
while the dissident duc d'Enghien is being sentenced to death
for conspiracy against the State, a kind of bugle call is heard
outside, along with a fart like the tearing of paper. That is

Beethoven ripping the dedication of the 'Eroica' to Bonaparte and announcing his opening theme, no longer to be permitted to glorify tyranny.

The second movement moves at a very leisurely pace, with no irritably rapid changing of scene. We are listening to a marcia funebre. N, in Moscow, has a nightmare of death by water, surrounded by derisive British tars. Simultaneously, though the dates deny it, Josephine dreams of becoming Queen of the Nile and, later, foam-born Aphrodite. Water is her element. Both she and N hear appropriate but ridiculous dream choruses, and these fit exactly the rhythms of Beethoven's main theme:

There he lies ensanguinated tyrant
See the reincarnate Cleo – patra

O bloody bloody tyrant See how the sin with–
Barge burning on the water Bare rowers row in

in Doth in– carnadine his skin from the
rows. Posied roses inter– pose twixt the

shin to the chin.
rows and the rose.

Beethoven's contrasting E flat major theme has significance, and terrible significance, for N only:

O Deutschland arise. Light is dawning in the Deutschlander skies.

When Beethoven recapitulates this theme, taking it nobly up to a B flat in the third bar, all that N's nightmare has to do is to add an *echt*. Not that he knows German. The text is able to throw whole lines from the libretto of *Die Meistersinger* at him, and he does not see the anachronism. Later a German, cousin of Stapps, who tried to assassinate him in the name of a rising Germany, commits the impossible solecism *Der Volk*. It should be *das*. There are two other such deliberate errors in the symphony – false notes. Macdonald is made Irish, not Scots; the Balcombes are turned into Bascombes. The reader should be uneasy about the presence or absence of an S. *Es* is the German for E flat. The invariable key signature of the symphony is being affirmed. This goes too far. Give us, etc.

Beethoven goes into a C major episode with rippling arpeggios, stepping into it, indeed, with a G, A and B. N steps into a boat on the Niemen to confer with Alexander, Tsar of all the Russias. The tranquillity of triumph remembered changes to the desperate urgency of a double fugue. Two bridges, N and J, have to be built for the *fuga* or flight of the Grand Army across the Berezina and out of Russia. One may not ignore the demand of the structure for verbal counterpoint:

Apprise the men of the inevitable difficulties of the constructive task that lies ahead, laying particular emphasis on the need for the utmost in improvisatory skill and stressing the importance of speed, General Eblé said, and the maintenance of sangfroid in the face of almost certain enemy harassment. Sergeant Rebour said: Right, lads, as you know, we lost the fucking pontoon train at Orsha, and all we have is a couple of field forges and a couple of wagons of charcoal and six truckloads of nails. He says he wants three bridges but I don't see how we can make him more than two. The primary need, General Eblé said, is to obtain the requisite structural materials and this will certainly entail the demolition of civilian housing in the adjacent township. Now the first job, Sergeant Rebour said, is to get planking, and the only way to get it is to pull down all those fucking houses.

And so on, for several pages, an alternation of officialese and demotic which, after the reading, it is hoped, will leave an aftertaste of polyphony.

The scherzo is both the simplest and most complicated problem of the entire book. Simple, because the A-B-A structure is

dedicated to mere play (hence the generic name) and the author
may forget the agony of finding correspondences and himself
play with language. Complicated because of the simplicity: playing the reprise is a mere matter of turning back the page and
repeating da capo; contriving a literary reprise becomes a head-
ache of describing N's escape from Elba, return to France, final
trouncing at Waterloo, in the same tropes and with the same
images as were initially appropriate to the Emperor's coronation
anniversary. Here is the opening:

From bivouac to bivouac to bivouac to bivouac to bivouac and all the
way it was torches held aloft with Long Live the Emperor and It Is
The Anniversary Of His Crowning and God Bless You Sire, rough
soldiers in tears of love and joy as he walked, with straw torches blazing
all about, from bivouac to bivouac to bivouac. He waved his hand in
thanks, tears in his own eyes, God Bless You My Children, and came
to the bivouacs of the artillery. Thank You Thank You he cried almost
weeping at the soldiers' tears and the fiery blessing and then:
    'Keep those fucking torches away from the artillery caissons.'

And here is the reprise:

From Cannes (has kissed the soil of France) to Grasse to Séranon to
Digne and there was no imperial eagle for the battalion from Elba to
set winging from belfry to belfry to belfry all the way to the pinnacles
of Notre Dame until they managed to knock a rough bird together from
bits of an old four-poster bed. He did not touch Fréjus on this return
journey since there had been no cries of Long Live the Emperor there
or God Bless You Sire, no woman's weeping, man's too for that matter;
instead there had been vulgar execration and even burning in effigy.
Over the Alps then with Thank You Thank You and God Bless You
My Children to those who brought him, Father Violent, Violet one
would say, Hope Of A Second French Spring, bunches of votive violets.
To the peasant who said he would sell him a horse for one thousand
francs (and there were only eighty thousand for the entire expedition)
he said:
    'Fuck you my friend and may your wretched nag be stricken with
the bog spavin.'

There is the same rhythm and much of the same phraseology,
culminating in the same obscenity, but whether this will be
accepted, even by the kindest musical reader, as the equivalent

of a repetition is doubtful. There are some things that words are not permitted to do.

Beethoven's scherzo seems, with its fiery strings and hunting horns, to be resurrecting the dead hero as Prometheus. In my trio I present a stage play in verse on the myth, but this is converted into a mocking British music-hall song:

The Continental System didn't work too well,
And the Spanish experience was concentrated hell.
Alexander promised friendship but decided to rebel
So I thought I'd quell the Russians with my shot and shell.
But we limped back from Moscow feeling sad and sore
And we had to meet Coalition Number Four.
We were trounced at Leipzig very very hard,
And now I am the Emperor
(Vive l'Empéreur)
Of an empire not much bigger than a knacker's yard.

The waltz rhythms of the imperial celebration are similarly mocked by the waltz rhythms of the Congress of Vienna. Marie-Louise's betrayal of her lord is expressed in the same Viennese dishes as her former gormandizing loyalty exacted: *Guglhupf mit Schlag, Bauernschmaus, Topfenpalatschinken*. The battle of Waterloo is raced through in a couple of pages. 'Horns and trumpets in hollow hunting harmonies, drums drums drums' celebrate an allied victory. Beethoven's and my scherzo meet only in an identity of orchestration.

I felt on safer ground with the finale. Beethoven begins with a rapid grandiosity matched by a rapidity of grandiose reminiscence as N approaches St Helena. *'Egypt 18 brumaire coup 3 cons 1st con 1st con for life exec of duc denghien Emperor Emperor EMPEROOOOOOOOOR.'* His island of exile is named for the Romano-British saint who found the true cross. Christ died, but Christ lives. N is removed from the worldly scene but his charisma cannot be quelled. Christ had INRI on the titulus of his cross. INRI can stand for *Imperatorem Napoleonem Regem Interfeciamus*. The initials and the whole phrase can be brokenly sung to the theme of Beethoven's variations (which, you will remember, comes straight from his *Prometheus* ballet music):

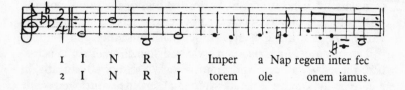

| 1 | I | N | R | I | Imper | a Nap | regem | inter fec |
| 2 | I | N | R | I | torem | ole | | onem iamus. |

INRI will keep appearing as an acrostic whenever the text breaks into verse. The variations find a literary counterpart in parodies or pastiches of the styles of British writers from Jane Austen to Henry James. N makes a friend of Betsy Bascombe in prim Regency prose. The *Edinburgh Review* provides a sneering fantasy on the significance of the letter W – which appears in *Wellington, Waterloo, Longwood* and *Lowe* – in the downfall of the Corsican tyrant. Sir Hudson Lowe, N's detestable jailor, appears as Sir Hud and N as Lion of the Valley in a logomachia in Sir Walter Scott's style. William Wordsworth, in blank verse out of *The Prelude*, sees N making a garden. The garden has become a symbol of the Napoleonic order imposed on Europe. The *spada* (sword) has been exchanged for a spade. Sergeant Trouncer and Private Slodge discuss N's failing health in the manner of Dickens. In Bulwer Lytton's prose the affair with Anna Walewska is recalled. N is feverish, he needs all that Polish snow. The Beethoven theme becomes distorted:

> K.N.V.S.
> KLEBA?
> NIEMA.
> VOTA?
> SANA.

The French troops in Poland ask for bread. There is none. Water? None of that either. Soon N becomes a thing, a recumbent comatose body. Dr Arnott, of the British medical fraternity, tries to feed this body milk; Dr Antommarchi, a Corsican of fierce Napoleonic loyalty, accuses the British of trying to poison their patient. The delirious N refights the battle of Austerlitz on his own swollen belly. A ponderous passage in Ruskinian style tells of a great storm blasting N's garden. 'Of all that he had made of green and grateful, of all that Nature, in her most complaisant dispositions, had afforded him of the same, nothing was to be left. There seemed to be lesson here, and it was that a man may not make even a garden with impunity.'

Tennyson, in *In Memoriam* style and stanza, with INRI acrostics, records N's death and mourns it. We join N after death, in a garden, talking to a young woman about the nature and value of heroism. The manner is that of Henry James, counterpointed with tropes from Gerard Manley Hopkins. War, says the unknown lady, is highly wasteful. If we need the heroic spirit we had best express it in art. N starts to be swallowed up in Beethoven:

. . . but of course *ce petit meinherr* had known, in his own way, and notwithstanding a disability that would not have gained him even the rank of plain *soldat*, all about the nature (the essence again!) of this particular glory, even though – and here was the deucedly queer thing – he evidently didn't go in at all much for that species of commodity. Thou mastering me. The chuckle, which had now become hard to control, went well enough with the music.

So the dead and corporal N is cut open for the postmortem, sewn up, buried. Betsy is Dickensianly tearful about him, Sir Hud permits only a blank tombstone without the 'legend of imperial pretensions', but, since Beethoven's finale ends with a blaze of E flat glory, N is evidently not dead after all. The whole dictionary rejoices – 'the bellowing gnu, ships and clarinets and tempests, the Son of Sirach, hazel and witch moth, cuckolds and warlocks, sorrel and alexia, Sir Thomas and Breslau and all the flowing wine of the world rejoiced. Rejoice. And again I say rejoice. And I say aga INRI ng bells bells bells bells and rejoice. Rejoice.' The most potent thing that Beethoven has given to the chronicler is the power to resurrect, since there is no real death in music.

I claim no originality for this use of the 'Eroica' as the matrix or template of a work of fiction: Galdos had got there before me with his four-volume novel and its carefully sculpted analogues of Beethoven. I can claim only that my aim, like Beethoven's and unlike that of Galdos, was to compress much into little; that the composer and I used the same subject matter is a theme for debate, since the 'Eroica' contains nothing but notes and the novel has a verifiable Bonaparte in it. The use of the term 'little' in connection with the symphony will seem inappropriate to some, especially the non-musical, to whom *symphony*, like *epic*, but not apparently like *saga*, conveys the notion of massiveness as well as supreme worth. Indeed, to entitle my novel *Napoleon Symphony* was called by some critics an act of presumption. A symphony and an epic are both, in comparison with a Dickensian or Jamesian novel, fairly short, and a tale of warriors is not necessarily ennobled by being told in verse, any more than sonata form canonizes the spinning of notes at Mannheim. My title makes a literal statement about the kind of shape I was trying to give to a historical narrative, no more. (Incidentally, that film was never made. A cinematic epic symphony on Napoleon can only be executed nowadays in the country which the re-arisen Emperor would gladly free from its Marxist tyranny.)

Does the artefact work? Is the concept viable? These questions are not to be asked. Most art is a failure, but art that does not risk failure is not worth attempting. (First sentence in a review: 'Mr Burgess's latest failure is entitled, somewhat grandiosely, *Napoleon Symphony*.') The general question may still be asked: can music teach anything to the novelist? Yes: the importance of structure. I mean variety of tempo, symmetry, the relating of subject to form. A simple example: if a character lights a cigarette on the first page, that must be balanced by the same, or another, character lighting one elsewhere, preferably on the last page. Themes must not be presented and abandoned. There must be development and free fantasy. The fictional structure must be planned in terms of how much space to give to what. Phrases and sentences should be framed in terms of a satisfyingly new, even strange or eccentric, sonic impact. If I am remembered for nothing else, I should like to be remembered for one sentence: 'He breathed bafflingly on him, for no banquet would serve, because of the known redolence of onions, onions, onions.' Dialogue should always sound natural – it is outside the reach of the influence of music – but the *récit* should be able to play melodies occasionally. There is too much grey prose about. Not even Brahms is grey, though he is muddy brown. The novel, like the symphony, is meant to be heard, but it is also meant to be seen. The 'Eroica' is not just noise on disc, it is the printed score as well. No one can judge a piece of music by merely hearing it; no one can judge a novel just by reading it.

I finish these few pages in the village of Callian in the Var district of Provence. I am in an old mill with paper and a typewriter and a few books. It is 14 July, and the *kermesse* is ended; the local band – piano accordion, electric guitar and alto saxophone – has just played the *Marseillaise*. Deryck Cooke, who has exhaustively inquired into the nature and operation of the language of music, hears in the opening phrase of that anthem a formula of awakening, girding one's loins, starting a new day. The same sequence of notes – low dominant, tonic, supertonic, high dominant – wakes the city in Vaughan Williams's 'London' Symphony and the woodwind in Sibelius's Fifth. Three different composers have attached the same meaning to the same basic theme. But how about Leonard Bernstein, with his song about New York being a hell of a town? He got his opening formula from Marseilles, or London, or Helsinki. Music is not inert and arbitrary, but it is not iconic either. We do not know what it is, except a great and sustaining mystery. I do not think we know what literature is either.